DISSECTING THE ACT

2009 POCKET EDITION
A UNIQUE STUDENT PERSPECTIVE ON THE ACT

By

Rajiv Raju

and

Silpa Raju

Platypus Global Media

Publisher:

Platypus Global Media

920 Naples Ln

Woodridge, IL 60517

 U.S.A.

For comments and information about additional copies Email:

dissectingact@yahoo.com

First Pocket (5.5" x8.5") Edition Published January 2009

ISBN: 978-0-578-00714-4

This pocket edition has the same content as the other edition of this
book, but it is printed in a slightly smaller format.

Other edition (6" x 9") of this book: ISBN: 978-0-578-00829-5 .

The 6"x9" edition distributed globally January 2009.

CONTENTS

Notes

PREFACE

The authors created this book to provide an inexpensive and concise resource to help students improve their ACT score. Most high school students are very busy and they can not devote too much time to ACT test preparation. Whatever time they spend for preparation should be spent using resources that are relevant to the real test, not on books that contain irrelevant and inaccurate representations of the test. The focus of this book is entirely on the *real* test. While the ACT expects you hove some factual knowledge of mathematical concepts, grammar concepts and punctuation rules, there is a great deal of emphasis on thinking skills. In fact the ACT Reading and Science Reasoning sections do not require any specific knowledge. Even the English section has a large number of rhetorical skills questions that can not be answered with knowledge of grammar rules alone. The Mathematics section also has many questions which require the application of concepts in novel ways. These questions test higher order thinking skills that can not be easily summarized. The only way to improve these skills in the short run is to practice and analyze real test questions. **This book provides specific information about how to get free access to three full real ACT tests, with a total of 645 real test questions.** The authors provide a detailed analysis of one of these tests. In addition, the authors have identified and listed the most essential factual knowledge that is necessary for success on the ACT test. The reader should find this work to be unlike anything else on the market.

Rajiv Raju and Silpa Raju

South Barrington, IL

January 2009

AUTHORS

Rajiv Raju is a student at Barrington High School (IL) at the time of publication. He wrote the Mathematics, Science and Reading sections of this book. He wrote this book to create an inexpensive resource to prepare for the ACT. Using strategies summarized in this book, he scored 35 or higher on all four sections of the ACT. In his free time, Rajiv likes to play Indian classical violin. He also likes to play the electric guitar and enjoys listening to his large and eclectic collection of music. He also enjoys reading suspense novels.

Silpa Raju is also a student at Barrington High School (IL) at the time of publication. She wrote the English and Writing sections of this book. She has not yet taken the ACT in high school. However, she did take the ACT in the 7th grade to qualify for summer programs and scored a 33 on the English component of the ACT at that time. More recently she scored a 770 on the Writing component of the SAT reasoning test, which tests many of the same concepts as the ACT English test. In her spare time, Silpa enjoys singing opera music and Indian classical music.

INTRODUCTION

Why another ACT test prep book?

There is no shortage of ACT test preparation books on the market. Almost all of these books, with the exception of the book from the test makers, have one very serious shortcoming: they attempt to create ACT type test questions. More often than not, these questions are not accurate representations of the real exam. Many of these books have irrelevant and inaccurate material and often have questions that do not have the correct level of difficulty. Making real ACT questions requires enormous resources that only the test makers have. This book makes no attempt to make up simulated questions, but instead focuses on an analysis of real ACT questions for one complete real ACT examination- dissecting the test, in other words. This complete real ACT test is available free of charge from the test maker. This analysis is performed by authors who have actually taken the ACT and have obtained high scores. In addition, the analysis of the test is from a student's perspective rather than from a teacher's or a test maker's perspectives. This unique perspective enables the authors to share insights not found in any other books. Using this book will give the reader a deep and accurate understanding of the skills and knowledge necessary for success on the real ACT test. This is the first step in maximizing one's score.

In addition to performing a detailed analysis of the official practice test, the authors have also evaluated other real ACT tests that are publically available and have identified the most important knowledge and thinking skills that are tested frequently on the ACT. These concepts are summarized for efficient review. Knowing the essential concepts is only the beginning; doing well on the ACT requires you to apply these concepts in ways that are often quite different from what is expected in school. In our opinion, the most effective preparation should include practice and analysis of real ACT questions. The next chapter includes a complete and detailed ACT test preparation plan that goes beyond this book and provides specific information about how to obtain three free real ACT tests.

Where do I get the real ACT questions?

The ACT provides a free booklet called <u>Preparing for the ACT</u>. It can be obtained for free at most high schools and directly from the ACT. The PDF file of this booklet can also be downloaded free from the ACT website at:

http://www.act.org/aap/pdf/preparing.pdf

This book assumes that you have the booklet released in 2006/2007, 2007/2008 or 2008/2009. As this book goes to press, we are not sure if the sample test will be the same for the 2009/2010 version of <u>Preparing for the ACT</u>. If you happen to get this book when the booklet with the current set of questions is no longer available from the ACT, contact the authors for the most current link to the PDF file of the booklet needed to use this book at:

dissectingact@yahoo.com

What about the book from the makers of the ACT?

<u>The Real ACT Prep Guide</u> which is made by the makers of the ACT is an excellent book and is highly recommended. This book has real ACT questions with explanations. Unfortunately it appears that the test makers do not want to give up too much specific information about what one is expected to know. For example, in the math content list on page 50 and 51 of the book, you will see a very general list of topics that is not very helpful. Under the trigonometry category "trigonometric identities" is listed. Are we expected to know all of the identities in the trigonometry book? <u>The Real ACT Prep Guide</u> does not explicitly tell you which specific formulas you must know. The authors of <u>Dissecting the ACT</u> have analyzed real ACT tests and identified what formulas and concepts the test makers expect you to know. The reader should find our book a useful complement to <u>The Real ACT Prep Guide</u>.

Organization of this book.

For each of the four major sections of the ACT, there is an introductory section which lists important content and skills needed for the section. There is also a strategy guide for the optional ACT Writing test, or essay. To illustrate how the concepts are tested, for some of the sections references will be made to real questions from the booklet, Preparing for the ACT. This is followed by an analysis of every question in the sample test. Some may feel that the content identified in this book is not comprehensive enough, but the objective of this book is not to be comprehensive- rather, it is to identify the concepts that are tested very frequently and therefore considered essential. The conventional wisdom is that a good high school education is the only comprehensive preparation for the ACT. While this may be true, the ACT only covers a small subset of what you learn in school. The most effective way to improve ones score is to understand what this subset of knowledge is and to understand how it is tested on the real ACT. The objective of the book is to identify the most frequently tested concepts and explain how they are tested by analyzing real questions.

Comparison with the SAT

Those who have prepared for the SAT should be aware of some important differences between the two tests. When dealing with the SAT there are debates about when to guess and when to leave an answer choice blank. On the ACT there is no debate about filling in answer choices. There is no guessing penalty on the ACT whatsoever. You should always fill in an answer bubble even if you did not read the question. The SAT usually has five answer choices, but most of the ACT only has four answer choices. This gives random guessing even more of an advantage. The Math section of ACT is the only section that has 5 answer choices. If you are running out of time and can not finish a section, make every effort to fill in an answer for each question.

Some parts of the SAT have easy questions at the beginning of the section and more difficult questions towards the end of section. There is no such order on the ACT. Never waste time on difficult questions. Guess and move on. If you dwell on difficult questions, you may not have time to attempt easy questions that may appear later on the test. This can hurt your score, and it is a shame to lose points on questions that you can otherwise answer if you get to them.

The ACT gives you significantly less time per question than the SAT. Correct pacing during the exam is *extremely* critical on the ACT. The English section has perhaps the most brutal time constraints, giving you only about 36 seconds per question on average! The math allots you a minute per question, making it the most generous section on the test. Both the science and reading give you slightly less than a minute to do each question. Most students who take the test seem to think that the time constraints are the biggest obstacle for them to overcome.

Although SAT is called the "Reasoning Test", the ACT also tests reasoning skills. In fact the "Science Reasoning" section on the ACT is almost entirely a reasoning test. The ACT English section tests all of the skills tested in the SAT writing multiple choice section, but also tests punctuation rules which do not show up on the SAT. The ACT math includes a few questions on more advanced topics, such as trigonometry. There is also the sporadic logical reasoning question, which can be answered with careful inference.

SUGGESTED ACT PREP PLAN

Save time and money- only use real tests!

We feel that effective ACT preparation should not require wealthy parents who are willing to pay hundreds, and in some cases thousands, of dollars for a prep class. We wrote this book to create an inexpensive resource that will let any person improve their score at least as much as a student in an expensive prep class can, if not more.

Get the free booklet <u>Preparing for the ACT</u> from your school or the ACT organization. You can also download it free form this link:

http://www.act.org/aap/pdf/preparing.pdf

Read the introductory portions of our book <u>Dissecting the ACT</u> and start doing the questions without any time limits. After doing each question, immediately read the explanation in our book that corresponds to that question. **Read the explanation even if you get the right answer**, since the explanations may give you insights that could help you with other questions. The objective is to really understand how the ACT tests your skills and how you can adapt your thinking to do well on the test. After going through all the questions in this booklet, <u>Preparing for the ACT</u>, you should have a very good idea of what it takes to get a good score. After doing this, go to this link:

http://www.actstudent.org/sampletest/index.html

There is another full free official test from the ACT at this link, and it even has explanations. While you do these questions pay attention to how long it takes to do the questions and see if you can develop your own strategies to increase your speed and accuracy. Identify any weak areas and go back and study the introductory content of our book. Following this, you can take a third free real ACT practice test under timed conditions. This test is available as a free download from the internet archive at this link:

http://web.archive.org/web/20050305184755/www.actstudent.org/pdf/preparing.pdf

You should now be ready to give the real ACT a try, but do not send the score to any colleges until you get the score that you are happy with. You can take the ACT multiple times and send the colleges your best score. The night before the test go over all the mistakes that you have made on the three real practice tests that you took so far.

If you are not happy with the score you get on your first try, get the book The Real ACT Prep Guide published by the test makers. This book has three more real ACT tests with explanations. You can buy this book new for about $16 on Amazon.com or get a used versions of this book via Amazon.com for about $5 including shipping. After taking the three tests in Real ACT Prep Guide, sign up for the test again and see how you do.

If you are still not happy with your score and feel that you need more practice with real tests, the ACT has an Online Course for $20. We have not taken this course, but we do know that includes two full real practice tests. We do not know how useful the rest of the course is, but the two official practice tests should be useful. After taking the two practice tests, sign up for the real test again. By now you have taken a total of 10 real ACT tests (8 at home and 2 for real) and you should be ready to ace the test. You have spent less than $50 on test prep, and should be at least as well prepared as those who have taken expensive courses.

ACT ENGLISH CONCEPTS
By **Silpa Raju**

The ACT English test requires much less grammar knowledge than what you may have learned in school. In fact, only a small subset of grammar concepts is repeatedly tested. The ACT never tests any grammar terminology. Since the ACT is locked into a multiple choice format, you are only required to recognize and correct poor use of language. However, in order to discuss the concepts that are tested on the ACT, it is necessary to introduce a limited amount of grammar terminology. The concepts described below are only intended for use on the ACT and may not be considered correct by your English teacher. The concepts will make much more sense when you see them used in real questions.

TERMINOLOGY

Noun- a person, place, thing or concept

Examples: John, Chicago, teacher, house

Pronouns- a subset of nouns that are used as substitute for another noun

Examples: I, you, he, she, it, we, they, me, you, him, her, us, them, one, which, that

Subject- a noun that does the action
Object- a noun that receives the action

Jane kicked the ball.

In this sentence above, Jane is the subject because she is the one kicking the ball, and the object is the ball, because the ball is being kicked.

Adjective- a word that modifies a noun

Example: Fast car. Fast modifies car.

Verb- an action word

Examples: sing, fall, scream

Adverb-modifies a verb, adjective or adverb

Adverbs can be identified most of the time by their ending: words ending in -ly are often adverbs.

Examples: kindly, gently, angrily

Article- a word that modifies or limits a noun

Examples: a, an, the

Phrase- a group of words that does not have both a noun and a verb at once and acts as a single part of speech.

Preposition – describes relative positions of ideas.

Jane put the book in the back pack.

The preposition is "in." The prepositional phrase is "in the back pack."

Clause-a group of words that have both a noun and verb

Independent clause- Has a complete thought and can stand alone as a sentence

Dependent clause- Has noun and verb, but can not stand alone as a sentence

SRTUCTURE AND GRAMMAR

A large portion of the ACT English section tests skills in sentence arrangement and parallelism. Let's move through all the structural errors tested on the ACT.

Errors in Sentence Structure

The comma splice

Two independent clauses can not be joined with only a comma, as in the following sentence:

He was too lazy to take down last year's calendar, it is still sitting there.

This sentence has a comma splice, but there are many ways to fix it.

We can add a period and make two sentences, like so:

He was too lazy to take down last year's calendar. It is still sitting there.

We can also add a conjunction after the comma.

He was too lazy to take down last year's calendar, so it is still sitting there.

We can even add a semicolon:

He was too lazy to take down last year's calendar; it is still sitting there.

Any of these fixes might show up as options in an ACT English test question.

The run-on sentence

A run-on sentence happens when two independent clauses are put together without punctuation. This is a run-on:

Sal wanted to go to the party he was grounded.

The run on sentence can be fixed with punctuation just like the comma splice, and can also be fixed with a conjunction.

Sal wanted to go to the part, but he was grounded.

Sentence Fragments

Fragments are just dependent clauses waiting to be completed. These do not form a complete thought, and they can not stand alone as a proper sentence. The following is a fragment:

When Donny was waking up.

To fix a fragment to make a grammatically correct sentence, you'll need to do one of the following:

Add an independent clause with a comma and a dependent clause:

When Donny was waking up, he realized he was late for work.

Taking away the word that makes this a dependent clause (when) :

Donny was waking up.

Parallelism and Agreement

Many ACT questions test parallelism/agreement in the form of tenses, plurality, etc.

Pronoun-Noun Plurality Issue

Every person who suffered through the period of the Black Plague certainly was thankful for their life.

In the above sentence, "every" is a singular word; therefore, the word "their" must also be singular.

Every person who suffered through the period of the Black Plague certainly was thankful for his or her life.

"His or her" is singular and now matches the plurality of "every".

Pronoun Usage: Subject or Object Pronoun?

In a sentence, you use certain pronouns to describe a subject and certain pronouns to describe an object.
Here are a few examples:

Subject Pronouns: he, she, it, they
Object pronouns: him, her, me, whom

Take a look at this sentence:

Me took a nap yesterday.

Since "me" is the subject, you should use a subject pronoun.

I took a nap yesterday.

Who/Whom

Probably one of the most baffling concepts for many test takers is the usage of who/whom. It's actually simpler than you think. The same rules about pronoun usage can be applied to the usage of who/whom. Try thinking of it in terms of she/her.

Who=she

Whom=her

(Who/whom) read the novel?

Her didn't read the novel, she did, so you would say who.

For (who/whom) should I buy a bouquet of flowers?

You would buy a bouquet for her, not for she, so you would say whom

Parallelism with Nouns and Verbs

When you see a series of nouns or verbs, be sure that they're all in the same tense or structure.

Noun parallelism

Though Larry was quite the intelligent student, he repelled a stereotypically nerdy persona with his sense of style, his street smarts, and his loving of things other than video games.

This might not sound incorrect, but if you look closely, there is a lack of parallel structure in the third listed phrase. "his loving" should be "his love" because "his love" would match the structure of "his sense" and "his street smarts"

Verb parallelism

Lisa had to do three things on this fine day: she needed to cook for her family, to go to an aerobics class, and picking up cash from the bank.

The same tense issue is present in this list of verbs. The first two verbs are in their infinitive form, ("to cook" and "to go") while the last verb is not. "picking" should be "to pick" to make it a parallel tense.

Incorrect placement of modifying phrase

A modifier phrase modifies another part of the sentence. The modifying phrase must be near the subject it is modifying to avoid confusion.

While reading a withered copy of Romeo and Juliet, fatigue came over Xiao.

This sentence reads like fatigue was reading Romeo and Juliet. Be sure to rearrange the sentence so it reads properly.

While reading a withered copy of Romeo and Juliet, Xiao was over come by fatigue.

While riding his bike, $150 dollars was found by Jim.

In the second incorrect example, its structure implies that the $150 was riding the bike!   Of course, we know that Jim was the one who was riding the bike and stumbled upon the $150.

While riding his bike, Jim found $150 dollars.

Agreement- Subject-Verb

A subject should agree with the verb in a sentence in terms of plurality.

Take a look at this incorrect example:

The part John hated most in the book were at the end.

In this sentence, the subject is "the part" and the verb is "were". Since the subject is singular, the verb must also be singular.

The part John hated the most in the book was at the end.

Now the subject and verb agree in plurality.

When pronouns are functioning as subjects, don't be fooled by their plurality.

Each of the chapters in the book have a title.

The subject is *ONE chapter* because the sentence says "each of the chapters" which is singular. Therefore, the verb "have" must also be singular.

Each of the chapters in the book has a title.

Now the verb "has" is singular and shares the same plurality with "each".

Adjectives vs. Adverbs

Recall the difference between adverbs and adjectives from the terminology section. Adjectives only modify nouns, while adverbs describe other parts of speech.

Lauren opened the door briefly.

This sentence is correct because the adverb "briefly" is describing "opened". Now look at this incorrect sentence:

Lauren's boyfriend, Lawrence, is kindly.

This sentence is incorrect because the adverb "kindly" should actually be an adjective because it's referring to the noun Lawrence.

Lauren's boyfriend, Lawrence, is kind.

The sentence is now correct because "kind" is an adjective.

PUNCTUATION

Commas

The ACT heavily tests your knowledge of comma placement. Let's review where to put them.

Commas are used to:

Separate more than two items in a list-

Jen's dog ran under the table, through the kitchen, and into a wall.

Separating parts of sentences-

Think independent and dependent clauses, as well as phrases.

Separating two independent clauses- When a sentence contains two independent clauses, they are often joined by a conjunction, if not a semicolon or other means of connection. Placing a comma before the conjunction is proper.

Incorrect: *Julian was out for a run when he saw a ring on the path so he picked it up and gave it to his girlfriend.*

Correct: *Julian was out for a run when he saw a ring on the path, so he picked it up and gave it to his girlfriend.*

Commas are used to separate a modifier phrase from the thing that is being modified.

Filled with excitement, Genevieve ripped open her ACT results, tearing the report in the process.

In the above sentence, a comma separates the modifying phrase "filled with excitement" from the subject being modified, Genevieve.

Commas are also used to separate parenthetical expressions.

Miguel, the star of the track team, won at state.

In this example "the star of the track team" is the parenthetical phrase since it can be removed and the sentence still makes sense. If removing a phrase significantly changes the meaning of a sentence, then it is not a parenthetical phrase and should not be separated with commas.

Semicolons

The semicolon is used to separate two independent clauses that are closely related. If you see the semicolon used anywhere else on the ACT, it is being misused.

Rachel was a big spender; she became more frugal when her parents cut off her allowance.

In this sentence, both halves are independent clauses that can stand alone. This is an appropriate use of the semicolon.

Colons

Colons are used to introduce a list at the end of an independent clause and can only be used at the end of an independent clause. The list may contain one or many items.

Neha counted up the new clothes she bought while shopping yesterday: two shirts, a pair of jeans, and perfume.

Apostrophes

Apostrophes can be used to indicate missing letters in a word. For example, you can use an apostrophe to shorten "I am" to "I'm". Such contractions must be memorized, but fortunately we use most of them in everyday talk. Apostrophes are also used to indicate possession.

Stuart's new car is very fast.

If possession applies to a plural noun ending in "s" then the apostrophe comes after the "s."

The meeting is in the students' lounge.

Wrong answer choices on the ACT often use superfluous apostrophes. The object being possessed must follow the word that has the apostrophe. If this is not the case then an apostrophe is not needed.

Rules are different for "its" and "it's".

The word " it's" means "it is."

The word " its' " is always incorrect. If you see " its' " with the apostrophe after the "s" on the ACT it is an incorrect choice.

The word "its" indicates possession. There is no apostrophe here.

Dashes

Use dashes like you would use parentheses. Use two dashes unless the parenthetical expression comes at the end of a sentence.

Carl took his vitamin pill- just like he does everyday- right after dinner.
Or
Carl took his vitamin pill- he always takes it after dinner.

RHETORICAL SKILLS

Rhetorical skills questions test ideas that can't be memorized, but require a bit of thinking. These questions often require some basic writing skill, not to actually write, but to know how to edit a passage. Here we'll go over some of the types of rhetorical skills questions present on the ACT English test.

Ordering Sentences/Paragraphs

The ACT will on occasion ask you to pick the best order for sentences or paragraphs. The best way to do this is to think about which parts flow best in what order. This is where writer's sense comes in. What is the most logical order for sentences or paragraphs to go in? Do they keep a consistent flow of thought with smooth transitions? Arrange the sentences or paragraphs in an order you think flows easily.

Strategy

The ACT will ask you to edit the passage to make it better. To help you more accurately answer these questions, identify the point of the passage itself and also the audience it serves. Think about what you are putting in/cutting out in terms of the purpose of the passage and the readers.

Redundancy

The ACT tests redundancy in sentences. If you see a sentence using two synonyms right next to each other, you can pretty much assume that you need to axe one of them.

My friend played online Internet games daily in the year 1996.

In this sentence, it is implied that online games are on the Internet, and that 1996 is a year.

My friend played online games daily in 1996.

This sentence eliminates the unnecessary wording.

Unclear Pronoun Reference

When you have a sentence with two nouns and you use a pronoun, it may be unclear as to which noun you are referring to.

Melvin and Chris are good friends, but he is nicer.

In this sentence, it is not clear who "he" is talking about. Make it clear by removing the pronoun altogether and inserting a noun.

Melvin and Chris are good friends, but Chris is nicer.

Transitions

Some questions will ask you to choose the best transition to complete a sentence. You'll need to know the meanings of the transitions, but most of them are used in everyday speech so it shouldn't be a problem. Here's an example:

Sandra missed home while she was at college, (but/because) she also enjoyed dorm life.

When picking a transition, think about what it means. "But" is introducing two viewpoints or ideas, while "because" is cause and effect. Look for key words in the sentence that hint at what is going on. In the sentence above, "also" is introducing another perspective. "But" is a transition that means two different ideas or viewpoints. "Because" is a transition that is used for cause and effect. Since "also" is showing a different idea and not the result of something, we can use the transition "but".

OTHER TIDBITS

Idiom errors

One error that can't really be taught is an idiom error. To solve such questions on the ACT, all you can do is acquaint yourself with the English language through exposure. Idiom error questions generally test whether you know to use the right preposition or not. Here's an incorrect example:

Oscar went of the car.

"Of" is certainly not the right preposition to use here.

Oscar went to the car.

This sentence employs the proper use of a preposition.

No change/Omit

The ACT gives you a couple of repeated options. It is important to not neglect these choices, like many test takers do.

-No change:

The "no change" option is present on most questions in the writing test. Don't make up an error that's not there- for about a fourth of the questions, there is nothing wrong at all.

-Omit the underlined portion:

The "omit the underlined portion" option is often seen in rhetorical skills questions. Sometimes, an extra sentence or phrase just isn't necessary, and the test writers want you to just get rid of unnecessary wording, hence this option- in fact, when this answer is available, it's correct more than 50% of the time. If you feel a passage could do without a sentence, cutting it out isn't a bad idea.

Notes

ACT ENGLISH TEST EXPLANATIONS
By **Silpa Raju**

Please refer to the questions in the English component of the practice test in official ACT booklet, Preparing for the ACT (2008/2009).

1) The concept being tested in this question is redundancy. Choice A, or no change, is wrong because "associated" and "connected" are synonyms, and only one is necessary to get the point across. Choice B, "connected by some of them", when put into the sentence, would read like this: "For some people, traditional American Indian music is connected by some of them with high penetrating vocals accompanied by a steady drumbeat". Although this sentence removes the redundancy of the first choice, it introduces a new error. The sentence has already noted the people who link traditional American Indian music with high penetrating vocals and a steady drumbeat, so the "them" in choice B is unnecessary and creates confusion. Choice C does not fix the error of redundancy in the first choice, because "linked" and "association" both mean to join. Choice D, however, removes redundancy by using one word, associated, and does not introduce any other errors. Therefore, **choice D** is the correct answer for this question.

2) This question requires rhetorical skills knowledge. There is no error with the sentence as it is. Choice G is incorrect because of the parenthetical phrase, "one might say". This phrase is irrelevant and unnecessary to the sentence. Choice H is wrong because "really quite popular" is unnecessarily wordy and confusing. Choice J can be eliminated because like the other choices, it contains more superfluous wording. **Choice F**, or no change, is the best choice because the sentence was correct as it was.

3) Question 3 tests punctuation. It asks which of the choices is NOT acceptable. If we look at choice, we see that it contains a semi-colon, so there is no error because it has eliminated the run on sentence we see in choice B, which separates two

independent clauses with a comma. Compound sentences, when joined by a comma, must consist only of dependent clause and a independent clause, where as this sentence tries to combine two independent clauses. Choice C separates the two independent clauses by putting them into their own sentences, thus separating ideas. Choice C, like choice D, avoids the error of a run-on sentence with a semi-colon, which correctly joins the two clauses. **Choice B** is the correct answer because it is creating an error.

4) Here you see a construction error. A construction error is when words are misplaced and they make a different meaning. In the phrase, "music that performed", it seems as though the music performed. To imply that it is a social music performed at weddings, you must get rid of the "that", because none of the choices involve an "is", which is necessary if you have a "that" in the phrase. Choice G is wrong because "music in which it is performed" does not work because the sentence would read: "It is a social music in which it is performed at weddings, birthday parties, and feasts." Here you are saying that the music is performed within itself, which makes no sense whatsoever. In choice H, music, performing, is not a suitable choice because of the –ing ending. You do not need an –ing in the phrase here, and generally, one should avoid –ing. It also sounds like the music is performing itself. **Choice J** is the only logical answer because "music, performed" uses the correct ending, -ed (past tense) and makes the sentence flow well, so it reads- "It is a social music, performed at weddings, birthday parties, and feasts." The commas correctly break the sentence.

5) Comma usage is being tested here. Choice B is not correct because it has too many commas; the use of a comma after "word" is unnecessary, as well as after "itself". Choice C doesn't work because again, the comma after "word" is not needed. Choice D is incorrect because no comma is necessary after "itself". Therefore, **choice A** is the best choice because it uses no unnecessary commas. In fact, it doesn't use any commas, because none are needed.

6) This question tests if you know how to fix the incorrect placement of a modifier. The phrase "Cheek to cheek, the

dance is performed to the relaxed two-stepped tempo" is incorrect. The modifier, or the part before the comma (cheek to cheek), is modifying what? Obviously it is not modifying the dance, but the people. The noun being modified should follow after the modifying phrase. So we can eliminate some choices from here- which ones don't have a phrase about persons immediately after the comma? Choice J doesn't, so we can eliminate that. If we look at choice H, we see that the modifying phrase before the comma is totally changed to "a relaxed two-step tempo". We can use our same principle here. What should "a relaxed two-step tempo" modify? The phrase has it modifying the couple, which makes no sense, so choice J is out. The only remaining **choice is G**, where there is no separated modifier, just a phrase, "Couples dance cheek to cheek to the relaxed two-step tempo". There is no error in this phrase, and it is the only remaining choice, so it is correct.

7) Like question 5, this question tests comma usage. If you look at choice B, you see unnecessary commas after "long" and "past", which makes the choice incorrect. Answer C also introduces excess commas, which are unnecessary after "play" and "past". Finally, choice D has an unneeded comma after "play", making it wrong. So, **choice A**, no change, is the correct answer.

8) This question tests whether you know your tenses or not. If we observe choice F, no change, we see that the word "were" is past tense, though the sentence itself is present tense because of "step", which is present tense. So we must find a choice that agrees with the present tense of this sentence. Choice H uses the word "have", which means they have already done it, so that wouldn't work. Choice J uses "will", which is future tense, making it wrong. **Choice G** is the only choice that uses a present tense verb, "are". The word fits the sentence because it is present tense.

9) Plural or singular? There, their, they're, its, or it's? The sentence is asking for a pronoun, so we need to pick the right one. Choice B isn't fit for the sentence because "they're" is an abbreviation for "they are", and the sentence, "As the dancers step to the music, they are also stepping in time to a sound that embodies their unique history and suggests the influence

of outside cultures on their music." would not make any sense. Choice C is singular, and we are looking for a plural pronoun because of the word "dancers", which is plural, so it is wrong. Choice D isn't a word, making it incorrect. The correct **choice is A**, because "their" is singular and is a fit pronoun to replace "dancers".

10) Here we see a rhetorical skills question. The writer of the passage wants to add the sentence "The agricultural practices of the O'odham are similar to those of the Maya.". In context of the passage, the last sentence of the paragraph 2 is "As the dancers step to the music, they are also stepping in time to a sound that embodies their unique history and suggests the influence of outside cultures on the music." The sentence of paragraph 3 says "The O'odham in the 1700s first encountered the guitars of Spanish missionaries." So, would the sentence about agricultural practices fit between those two? Probably not. One sentence is talking about dancing, while the other is talking about missionaries from Spain. So, armed with the knowledge that it doesn't fit, we can already eliminate choices F and G, because they state that it does fit. Look at choice H; it says that the sentence shouldn't be there because the author has not mentioned a connection between the Mayas and the O'odham. However, the author did mention that outside groups influence culture, so if he had said that the Mayas contributed to the culture surrounding waila, then it might have worked. However, to throw in a sentence about agriculture when you are talking about music and dancing is random, and distracts from the point. **Choice J** states just that, therefore making it correct.

11) This is a construction problem. If we look at the question, we see it asks which placement of the phrase would be wrong. Choice A, where it is, works because when we read the sentence as it is, it makes sense. Choice B is also correct, because it would read "In the 1700s, the O'odham first encountered the guitars of Spanish missionaries." and it follows all of our modification rules. Choice D is also correct because the sentence would say "The O'odham first encountered the guitars of Spanish missionaries in the 1700s." which makes perfectly good sense. Choice C is wrong because it would be like adding a random phrase into a sentence, which makes it confusing and distracts from the

point. Since we are looking for the wrong placement, **Choice C** is the right answer.

12) You will need to know your tenses to solve this one. This sentence is past tense. F is wrong because it unnecessarily uses "have" in front of the borrowed. Watch out for unnecessary "have" usage in sentences. Choice G is present tense, so that wouldn't work with a past tense sentence. Choice H, "were borrowed" is incorrect because it is implying that the O'odham were borrowed, when in fact the sentence is trying to get across the dancing that was borrowed, not the O'odham. **J is the simplest choice, as well as the correct one.** It uses past tense, and is very concise.

13) This is a construction question. They are asking which parenthetical phrases are most relevant to the paragraph. Answer B talks about fiddles being used in waila long ago. Although this may be a tempting choice, considering it has to do with waila, there is a better choice. Choice C says instruments are often made of metal, but does this have anything to do with the paragraph? We want germane information. Choice D says that these instruments are found frequently in jazz bands. This also has no relation to the passage. **Choice A** is the only correct choice because the phrase in the parenthesis, as it is, provides relevant information that aids the reader in understanding why there are saxophones in waila. This is the only information that the reader might need, out of all the choices.

14) In question 14, you are being tested on whether you know where to put punctuation. The sentence is actually fine without punctuation, making **choice G** correct. Choice F is incorrect because no semi-colon is needed there; semi-colons are used to separate two independent clauses, like conjoining two sentences into one. Choice H is also wrong because a colon signifies that a list is coming up. There is no list in this sentence. Choice J is incorrect because a comma is used here, where no pause is needed.

15) Here's another one of those rhetorical skills questions. It's asking which paragraph the sentence they give you would be best to put after. The sentence talks about German influences,

so we need to find where they say anything about Germans. It appears that paragraph 3's last sentence says that the Germans' music influenced waila. Paragraph 3's last sentence is the only place where they even say anything about Germans, making it the correct paragraph to put the sentence after. Therefore, **choice C**, paragraph 3, is the right answer.

16) This question does not test your grammar, like most questions on the ACT English Test. Instead, it tests your word choices. Which of the words fits best? Choice A, no change, wouldn't work very well because the difference between Korean years and American years is not a competition. G, or change, is also incorrect because, like contest, the Korean and American ways are different, not a change. H is also incorrect because a dispute is more of a fight, and this year-difference isn't a fight at all. **Choice J** is the correct answer because it uses the word "difference" in the sentence, which is exactly what Korean years and American years are like; different.

17) This question is testing if you know how to make parenthetical phrases. Choice A is incorrect because since there is a comma after "system", but this is meant to set off a phrase. In order to set off a phrase, you must have two commas, one at the beginning of the phrase and one at the end. C is also wrong because a colon signifies that a list is coming, and there is no list in the sentence. Finally, choice D is incorrect because "a person who, according …" wouldn't make any sense. A person who what? **Choice B** is the best answer because it uses a comma after "person" to complete the parenthetical phrasing by adding the starting comma.

18) This is a rhetorical skills question. This sentence really doesn't fit in the paragraph- We are talking about how the birthday system in Korea works, not about birthdays worldwide. We can eliminate choice F. Let's eliminate the other irrelevant choices. Choice G is also wrong because again, it is off topic and does not fit into the paragraph. Choice H is also wrong for the same reason as the other choices. Only **choice J** works, because it deletes the unnecessary sentence all together, making the paragraph stay on topic.

19) Here, we must pick the word that correctly describes the

"celebration" the author speaks of. "Heightened" could mean lifted, but in this case, it means "to show light upon". This would be an acceptable word for the sentence, making choice A correct. Choice B is incorrect because "raised", when put in this sentence, would mean literally lifted up. If you said something like "raised importance" or "raised awareness" that would make more sense. Choice C is also incorrect because "lifted" means to physically pick something up. Choice D is wrong because "lighted" wouldn't make sense in the sentence- instead you would have to say "shed light upon". **Choice A** is the best answer.

20) We must identify what the passage would lose if the author were to delete the preceding sentence. Choice G is incorrect because the sentence doesn't talk literally about what happens at birthdays, it's just talking about what New Year's could be thought of. Choice H is also wrong because the sentence isn't defending anything, and there is no case in the passage; the passage is simply comparing the American system of birthday counting to that of the Korean system, not trying to choose which is better. Choice J is incorrect because the sentence isn't actually talking about the Korean counting system at all- once again, it is talking about the importance of New Year's Day and the celebration. Notice how all of the choices, except choice F, are incorrect because they don't relate to the sentence the question is referring to. **Choice F** is the best answer because it talks about the "significance" of the celebration, which is exactly what the sentence is talking about.

21) Question 21 is similar to question 19- they both ask you to choose the right word. The sentence needs a word or words that support a point. Choice A, otherwise, would be used to compare two things. Answer B is also used to compare things; though this, that. Choice D is used to talk about something in the past. None of these help to support a point, so **C is the best answer** because "in fact" is adding another significant point to the argument.

22) Idiom-usage is being tested here. Choice G is wrong because "on" means "above" or "upon", so that wouldn't make much sense with "point". Choice H is also wrong because "at" is the

wrong preposition- "point to" is the better preposition. Choice J, or deleting the preposition all together, would disrupt the sentence's flow by removing an essential preposition. **Answer F is the only correct choice** because "point to" uses the correct preposition. Remember that idioms are solid rules that you have to follow- you cannot explain why "at" is the wrong preposition and "to" isn't, for it is just an idiom-usage rule.

23) This question tests punctuation and plurality. Choice B is incorrect because the word "a" is talking about one person and the noun "persons" is plural. Choice C is also wrong because, again, "persons" is plural, and "a" is singular. Choice D is wrong, not because of plurality, but because it introduces another error. It adds an unnecessary comma after the phrase "person's age" and no pause in the sentence is needed there. The only acceptable **choice is A**, because person's age is singular and has no other punctuation errors.

24) Here we are tested on pronoun usage. In order to use a pronoun in a sentence, it must be referring to someone or something. In this sentence, who is "their" referring to? This makes choice F incorrect, because we do not know who "their" is. Choice G is also incorrect because "one's" idea could mean anyone. Choice H is wrong because "it's" is referring to an object or creature. This sentence is not in need of a pronoun, because it does not refer to anyone or anything in particular. **Choice J** is the only correct answer because "this" is not a pronoun.

25) You should know your idiomatic expressions for this question. It's hard to explain to you why any of the answers are wrong, for idioms have no rules; they are just the way they are. All of the choices except B are the wrong words to make this idiom work. **Choice B** is the best answer.

26) This is a rhetorical skills question. Which choice best implies the elders' positive attitudes towards the practice of adding a year? Choice G means basically "doing what everyone else does", so that's not the best answer. Choice H is wrong because "living with two birthdays themselves" doesn't really imply any positive connotation. Choice J is also incorrect because "obligingly" means "doing as you're told". **Choice F,**

"with great enthusiasm", definitely implies a positive connotation, because of the use of "enthusiasm", which says that the elders enjoy adding a year to their age.

27) This question deals with an idiom as well as unclear pronoun reference. Choice B is not correct because "whose" refers to persons, not things (society). There needs to be a number agreement in the sentence. Choice C is also wrong because "this" is an idiom error. Choice D is incorrect because whom is referring to a person, not a thing (society). **Choice A** is the only correct answer because it uses the correct pronoun and refers to things, not people.

28) Your rhetorical skills are tested in this question. Choice F is incorrect because the sentence the question is referring to doesn't have a personal nor a reflective tone. Choice G is also wrong because the sentence isn't really humorous at all. Choice J is not correct because the writer does not express support for either side, the Korean way of counting or the American way of counting. **Choice H** is the only correct answer because the phrases the question talks about are relevant to show contrast between the young and the old.

29) You'll need to know some basic vocabulary for this question. Here, we want to choose the least repetitive choice. Choice A is incorrect because balk and refuse both mean the same thing, and you wouldn't hesitate if you refused, you would simply not do whatever is being asked. Choice B is also wrong because, like choice A, if you balked, you would not bother to hesitate, but instead refuse completely. Choice C is not correct because refuse and balk both mean the same thing, so you wouldn't have to have both. **Choice D** is the best choice because balk means to refuse, and eliminates repetition, while making sense unlike some of the other choices.

30) Which word would best imply that something is simple, but could prove to be a little difficult? Choice F is not correct because "visibly simple" means that it is most definitely simple, and does not imply that it could be potentially difficult. You might be tempted to choose this because visibly could mean on the outside, but there are better options. Choice H is incorrect because "entirely" also does not imply that there

could perhaps be any difficulty whatsoever. Choice J, "fully" also creates the same error as the other choices. **Choice G** is the word that would fit best into the sentence because "apparently" casts doubt upon whatever is being described, so when we say something is "apparently simple", we are implying that it may look simple, but that might not be the case. "Apparently" casts more doubt than "visibly simple" does.

31) Which of the answers best illustrates "dress code" in the sentence? If we look at the sentence, we see the words "certain types of clothing", so our ideal choice would have a list of certain types of clothing that aren't aloud in this "dress code". With this in mind, we can eliminate all the choices except answer C, which contains a list of clothing describing what the dress code would prohibit. When you give examples, it best supports whatever you are talking about. **Choice C** is the best answer.

32) For this question, you'll need to choose the best words to describe how the students act toward school work. Choice F, inefficient toward, doesn't make much sense- you would probably say inefficient with school work, not inefficient toward school work. Choice G does not keep a serious tone like the rest of the essay, nor does choice H. This makes **choice J** the best choice because it uses a serious tone, while describing just how the children would act toward school work.

33) We need a good introductory sentence for the paragraph. Choice B is probably not a good sentence to start a paragraph because the principal was not mentioned anywhere in the paragraph at all, and it doesn't matter what the principle said; the fact that Kevin Bannister violated the dress code is enough proof as to why he got sent home. Choice C is also a wrong answer because there is no support for the statement- again, the principle is mentioned nowhere in the passage. Choice D is incorrect because the statement is completely irrelevant. It doesn't matter whether this happened at a bad time or a good time. **Choice A** is the best answer because by leaving the first sentence as it is, you are introducing the paragraph and hinting at what will be in the paragraph. By telling that Kevin and his parents felt that their rights had been violated, you are

introducing that they were unhappy with the school, which leads into the lawsuit that follows.

34) Punctuation is being tested in this question. This phrase actually needs no punctuation, so we can eliminate all choices with punctuation, making **H the best answer**. Choice F is wrong because a colon signals that a list will follow, and there is no list in this sentence. Choice G is wrong because by putting a comma after "Court", you are putting in an unnecessary pause. Choice J is also incorrect because there is a comma, which puts in a pause that is not needed.

35) Idiomatic phrases are being used in this sentence. Once again, idioms are special rules that you must memorize. There is no explanation as to why one answer is wrong and the other isn't- its just the idiom's rule. Answer **C is the best choice** because "to" is the correct word to put before "wear". Notice that all verbs can have a "to" before them: to dance, to sing, to fall, to jump, to run. "Wear" is a verb, and therefore can have "to" before it, not for, thus eliminating choice A. Choice B, "of wearing" is incorrect because there is no need for an –ing after wear. Be cautious of –ing words on this test; they are often unnecessary and are there to confuse you. Choice D is wrong because you need to have some sort of transitional word between "right" and "wear".

36) In this question, you must know your comma rules. Choice F is incorrect because "however" needs to be set off by commas, for it is an unnecessary word within the sentence. There is a comma before "however" but not after, so it is wrong. Choice H is wrong because "noted however" is not the unnecessary word in the sentence; in fact, it is a phrase, not a word. Choice J is also incorrect because "however" has one comma after it, and you need two to set off a word/phrase- one before, and one after. **Choice G** is the best choice because it correctly sets off "however" by adding a comma before and after the word.

37) This question tests rhetorical skills. Edit out what you don't need. Choice A isn't- we don't really need to know that authority figures guided the educational process. Choice B is also off topic because the paragraph has nothing to do about

changes from the past. Choice C is incorrect because, well, the added "the process we all know well" just isn't necessary- and who says all of us "know well"? **Choice D** is the best answer because it makes the sentence concise and doesn't add any totally irrelevant phrases at the end.

38) You will need to know about contractions for this question. Choice F is wrong because "it's" is a contraction for "it is". The sentence needs the kind of "it" that implies possession. Choice G is also wrong because "they're" is short for "they are" and again, you need a possessive word, not one that uses "it" or "are" to follow up with a description. Choice J is also wrong because "ones" could mean anyone, not just the board. **Choice H** is the best answer because "its" is the possessive word that is singular, so you can use it on "the board" which is a singular noun.

39) You will see plenty of questions about idioms on the ACT, and here is just one of the many. Choice B is wrong because it uses the wrong word, and it doesn't satisfy the idiom, and so are choices C and D. **Choice A** is the one correct answer because it is the right word for this idiom. Once again, you'll have to memorize these rules of idioms- there are no tricks to figure it out.

40) Here is a rhetorical skills question. Choose the right word that hints at what will happen next. Choice G is wrong because "thus" isn't a good word to use here- you can't set off "thus" with commas. "Thus" must be followed by a verb. H is also wrong because "moreover" implies that there is a bigger reason, but the sentence doesn't announce a bigger reason for the court's decision. Answer J is also wrong because "however" implies that there is something opposite from what is going on. "However" could imply irony, something bad if things are good, something good if things are bad, etc.- pretty much any opposition. There is no opposition between the court and anyone else in this particular sentence. The answer is **choice J**.

41) We need to use the correct tense and idiom in the sentence. Choice A uses the correct tense by using –ing, but uses the wrong word for the idiom. Choice B is wrong for the same

reason. Choice D is using the wrong tense- worn is past tense, and we need a present tense verb. **Choice C** is the best answer because it uses a present tense word and eliminates the unnecessary idiomatic phrase.

42) This is another rhetorical skills question. Pick the choice sentence that shows how important Kevin's case is. Choice G Is a reminder to you, not a statement that conveys importance. Choice H is talking mostly about the courts, and not specifically about the case. Choice J is wrong because again, it does not illustrate the importance of the case. **Choice F** is the best answer because it directly states "Kevin Bannister's case was significant", which is what the question asks for.

43) Punctuation is being tested in this question. **C is the best answer** because the phrase does not need any commas, and C is comma-free. All the other choices unnecessarily use commas to create breaks in the sentence, which is not needed.

44) This is an idiom error, where you need to pick the correct preposition. Choice G probably isn't the best answer because on literally means "above" or "on top of", so that wouldn't work. Choice H means "together" so that isn't the best choice either. Choice J means "has to do with" and that wouldn't fit too well with the sentence. The best answer would be **choice F**, because "in" public education implies "in the area of public education", which is exactly what we are looking for.

45) This is another rhetorical skills question. Did the essay try to persuade students to exercise their rights? Not really. Choice A is incorrect because Kevin Bannister didn't actually do anything to persuade other students to make full use of their rights. Choice B is wrong because the essay only focuses on Kevin, and no other students. Choice C is also incorrect because the essay does not suggest that the right to wear blue jeans wasn't significant. The whole essay is based on the violation of Kevin's right to wear blue jeans, implying that it is quite important. **Choice D** is the best answer because the essay does only talk about one student, Kevin Bannister, and explains his constitutional right that was violated. The essay does not persuade others to make use of all their rights, but

instead tells the story of an unfair punishment that violated one's rights.

46) This is a construction question. Choice F doesn't really fit in the blank too well because "since" in the context of this sentence would mean "from then onward", and we aren't talking about what has happened from the past to the future. Choice H is incorrect because "concerning" means "having to do with" and we already know it has something to do with this belief of his. Choice J is just wrong idiom-usage. **Choice G** is the best answer because "because of" implies that because of this belief, he was fooled by these girls.

47) Here's a rhetorical skills question. What would the essay lose if the author deleted the first sentence of the paragraph? Answer B is incorrect because there are no humorous parts of the essay, and the sentence isn't irrelevant. Choice C is wrong because the first sentence does not explain Sir Arthur Conan Doyle's motivations at all- it questions something you may think about him. Choice D is also incorrect because the sentence does not describe any setting. **Choice A** is the correct answer because the sentence does set up a contrast- the first sentence says you may think he is a logical person but the next sentences starts with a "but", introducing a contrast, and then tells how he believed in mythical creatures and fantasy, which are not very logical. The "but" is a very key word here, for it tells the reader that there is a contrast coming.

48) This question also deals with plurality. Answer F is incorrect because "girl's" is singular, while "faces" is plural. Choice H is wrong because it does not have an apostrophe in the word "girls" to show possession, of in this case, a face. Choice J is also incorrect because the apostrophe is placed in the word "face's" and the girl has possession, not the face. **Choice G** is the best answer because the apostrophe is placed appropriately after "girls", which shows that the girls have possession, while sticking to plurality rules.

49) Try and avoid redundancy here, and be concise. In choice A, "true" and "factual" basically mean the same thing, so that choice is redundant, making it incorrect. In choice B, "evident" and "apparent" are the same, and you don't need the "but"

because there is no comparison, making it wrong. Choice C is long and unnecessary. **Choice D** is best because "this apparent" best gets the point across, while hinting at a bit of skepticism and being concise.

50) We need to use the right pronoun here. In choice F, the "however" makes a run on sentence. Choice H is wrong because it refers to an item or object, and choice J is wrong because it makes a run-on. **Answer G is correct** because because "who" refers to people and does not make a run on. This is another rhetorical skills question. Do keep in mind, however, that the shortest answer is not always the best answer. Choice A is incorrect because the answer is extremely long and unnecessarily complicated. The word "being" just sounds weird. D can also be eliminated because of this of an idiom error dealing with "where". Choice B is wrong because "in which the magazine where" does not make sense because the sentence has already acknowledged the fact that the article is in a magazine and is telling location twice unnecessarily. In addition, you do not need to write "in which" and "where" in this phrase twice because they serve the same purpose- to tell where the article was put. **Choice G** is the correct answer because "in which" correctly tells where the article was and is short, introduces no grammatical errors, and does not sound eccentric.

51) This is another rhetorical skills question. Do keep in mind, however, that the shortest answer is not always the best answer. Choice A is incorrect because the answer is extremely long and unnecessarily complicated. The word "being" just sounds weird. D can also be eliminated because of this of an idiom error dealing with "where". Choice B is wrong because "in which the magazine where" does not make sense because the sentence has already acknowledged the fact that the article is in a magazine and is telling location twice unnecessarily. In addition, you do not need to write "in which" and "where" in this phrase twice because they serve the same purpose- to tell where the article was put. **Choice C** is the correct answer because "in which" correctly tells where the article was and is short, introduces no grammatical errors, and does not sound eccentric.

52) This is a fragment error. There is a phrase containing background information on Houdini that needs to be set off by commas. If you look after "Houdini" you will see a comma. This is the first comma used to set off the phrase, but you need a second at the end of the phrase to complete setting it off. This question is testing if you know where to put it and if you know what word to use immediately after to let the sentence flow. Choice F and J are wrong because they contain no comma at all. Choice G is incorrect because you need to put a verb after the comma, and "being" is not a verb. **Choice H** is the right answer because it puts a comma after the last word of the phrase, "spiritualism", and uses a verb directly after.

53) What would this essay lose if we omitted the sentence about Houdini being skeptical of supernatural beings and fantasy creatures? A is wrong because the sentence has nothing to do with the friendship of Houdini and Sir Arthur Conan Doyle. The sentence contains background information on Houdini's beliefs. Choice C is also incorrect because this sentence doesn't actually state reasons for Houdini's beliefs, but tells about Houdini's beliefs. Choice D is wrong because the sentence is significant, for it talks about Houdini's interest in solving hoaxes and reveals the reason why Sir Arthur Conan Doyle probably sent the picture to him- to see if they were real or not. **Answer B** is the correct because the sentence first tells Houdini's point of view on the matter, which is negative, and then the next sentence states how Houdini thought the pictures to be false.

54) This question is testing punctuations and transitions. Choice F is incorrect because you can't have "but" and "though" in the same sentence because they both convey contrast or opposition. G and H are also incorrect because when you use though at the beginning of the sentence, it calls for a comma at the end of the phrase because it is a dependent clause. **J is the right answer** because it contains a comma and does not repeatedly use words to show contradiction.

55) This is a rhetorical skills question. So, let's pick the least concision-challenged choice that is still legitimate. This is obviously not B because you shouldn't use "of the fact that" after "because" because you can shorten the sentence by

removing this phrase. Notice that "because they had a disagreement" makes more sense and is much shorter because of the removed "of the fact that". Choice A is also incorrect because of the whole the-fact-that-they-had thing, which is even longer than the phrase above. The sentence would also make sense if you said "due to the disagreement". Choice C is wrong for pretty much the same reason as A. **D is the best answer** because it is short and gets the point across without too many words.

56) This is rhetorical skills question testing organization. We will need to make this sentence a new paragraph because at the preceding sentence is talking about a disagreement between Houdini and Conan Doyle. This next sentence is talking about Frances Griffiths, exposing her own joke. They are two totally separate thoughts and need to be separated into different paragraphs. Therefore, we can eliminate choices F and G. H is wrong because you don't say "Since some" because since is unnecessary because it's already implied that it's "since" the incident. **Choice J** is the best answer because it is not redundant and separates the thoughts into different paragraphs.

57) Choose the right pronouns to use in this sentence. Choice A is incorrect because if we took away the extra subject, her cousin, that section would read "...admitted that her had staged the photographs as a practical joke." which would not make sense. For the same reason, we can eliminate choice B because "admitted that herself had staged the photographs" does not fit either. Choice D is also wrong for the same reason as B, except the compound subject is inverted so it reads "her cousin and her" rather than "her and her cousin". Either way, they are both wrong. **Choice C** is the right answer because if you removed either of the subjects from the compound subject, the sentence would still make sense. For example, if you removed "and her cousin", that part of the sentence would read "admitted that she had staged the photographs", whereas if you removed "she and" that part of the sentence would read "admitted that her cousin had staged the photographs".

58) This question tests your knowledge of tenses. Note that they are asking which answer would not be acceptable. There is

nothing wrong with choice F, G, and J. The only wrong **answer is H** because "using" is present tense, and the sentence is in past tense.

59) Chose the option that is related best to the opening sentence of the essay. The opening has Sherlock Holmes in it, so **B would be the best answer** because it also has Sherlock Holmes in it. Choice A has nothing to do with the first sentence, Choice C talks about Houdini, who wasn't in the first sentence and choice D also has nothing to do with the first sentence.

60) This is a rhetorical skills question testing your understanding of the essay. So did the essay successfully show how belief in the supernatural affects the works of authors? No, because they didn't really talk about or give specific examples of Doyle's writings being significantly changed by his belief in mythological creatures. This renders choices F and G wrong. Choice H is also wrong because no where in the essay does it say specifically that his belief in fairies and the supernatural didn't influence his writing. The essay does not argue this at all. **Choice J** is correct because the essay keeps the topic around how one author (Doyle) responds to the possibility of supernatural beings.

61) This is a pronoun error. Choice A is wrong because "whose" would make the part of the sentence after the comma a clause, when it has to be independent to make a complete sentence. Choice B is also incorrect because the sentence is talking about "her", not "them" and the given answer choice "their" is plural, and referencing "them". Choice D is wrong for the same reason as A. **Choice C** is the correct answer because the phrase containing "her" now has a subject to talk about, and the subject is also showing possession like the sentence requires, and is also singular.

62) This question tests punctuation. Answer G is wrong because using "and" is inappropriate. The phrase "and over one thousand letters to upwards of one hundred correspondents" needs a verb to make sense; that choice would only work if they had incorporated something like "were sent" after. Choice H is wrong because semicolons are used to break complete

sentences. Choice J is wrong because "Over one thousand letters to upwards of one hundred correspondents" is a fragment. **Choice F** is correct because the original sentence uses a colon. Colons are used in front of a list or definition of the preceding word or phrase. The section after the colon is defining correspondence.

63) This question is testing rhetorical skills and punctuation. Choice A is incorrect because although a new paragraph need not be made, there should be a comma after woman. Choice C is incorrect because you don't need to make a new paragraph- the topic sentence is "Dickinson's lifetime..." and the next sentence fits perfectly, going into detail about how different periods of time had different tone of letter. Also, there is a comma inappropriately placed after "wrote". We can also eliminate choice D because you don't need to make a new paragraph. **Answer B** is correct because it doesn't start a new paragraph, and there are no punctuation errors.

64) This is an idiom error. Answer G is wrong because "to" should not be used where it is and it is unnecessary. Answer H is incorrect because it is not in the same format as the other example given- "of pinning for a valentine" does not say "of her pinning for a valentine". The "her" is unnecessary. For the same reason, Choice J is incorrect. The **correct answer is F** because it is simple and follows the same format as the preceding example.

65) This is another rhetorical skills question. Which answer tells how the letters played a role in Dickinson's life? Choice A only talks about the time range she wrote to others, not what effect they had on her. Choice B is also incorrect because it is off topic and unrelated to the letters. Answer C is wrong because it does not tell you about how her life was affected, but only that her letters were revealed after death. **Choice D** is the best answer because it tells you how the letters affected her personally- she enjoyed hearing her friends' news and reflections on political events.

66) This is a punctuation question. F is incorrect because a semicolon breaks the sentence incorrectly, and "speaking of relatives and friends whom had died" is a fragment and cannot

be put alone after a semicolon. G is also wrong because the sentence is past tense and "speak" is present tense, and it's also a run on sentence. Choice J is incorrect because "speaking of relatives and friends whom had died" is a fragment and can't be made into its own sentence. **Answer H** is correct because the comma correctly breaks the sentence and conjoins an independent clause with a dependent clause.

67) This question is testing your knowledge of who/whom. Reference the who/whom rules in the introduction. Who died? She died, not her, so you would use who. The correct **answer is B**.

68) Here's yet another punctuation question. The sentence does not need a break at all, and all the answers except for G have breaks in them, so they are all wrong. **G is the correct** answer because it has no breaks, and the sentence doesn't need them.

69) In this question, unclear pronoun reference is being tested. Answer A is incorrect because "her" does not specify that Susan is giving Emily feedback- it instead sounds like Susan is giving herself feedback. Choice B is also wrong because the "her" is placed before "Emily", which still causes confusion because since "Emily" is not placed first, so the "her" has nothing to describe. Answer D is incorrect because this choice makes no effort to solve the issue at hand- directing the pronoun to the noun it's taking the place of. The right answer is **choice C** because "Emily" is placed before "her", so the pronoun "her" has a noun to describe.

70) Here's a rhetorical skills question. For this question, you have to find the ending that is most relevant to the sentence. All of them are grammatically correct. However, all the choices are incorrect except J, because they don't have much to do with what is being talked about in the paragraph. The only logical answer from the choices **would be J** because it ends with a period, and does not add any unnecessary ending, like the other answers.

71) This is another rhetorical skills question. In this question they are asking which choice illustrates an interaction between

Susan and Emily the best. Choice A is incorrect because even though Susan read the poem, this does not show any sort of interaction between her and Emily. Answer B is also wrong for the same reason as A. Susan may have liked the poem, but that doesn't show her communicating with Emily. C is incorrect for the same reason as A and B. **Answer D** is the best answer because it depicts Susan actually communicating with Emily by suggesting revisions.

72) Redundancy is being tested here. In many cases, though not all, the shortest choice is the best choice. This applies to this question. Answer G is wrong because "other" and "alternate" are synonyms, and therefore you do not need both. Choice H is also incorrect because "alternate" and "additional", in the way "additional" is being used, are synonymous. And J is also wrong because it can be inferred that the alternate versions are revised, so it is unnecessary to use both "alternate" and "revised" in the sentence. **The best answer is F** because the phrase "wrote two other" is understandable and simple and gets the point across without too much trouble.

73) Here, a couple of topics are being tested. Choice A is incorrect because "letters" and "reveals" do not agree in number- "letters" is plural and "reveals" is singular. Don't be fooled by interjecting phrases like in this sentence- the test tries to trick you here by separating a noun from its action. Answer C is wrong because the passage is past tense, not future tense, and "will" usually indicates future tense. D is incorrect because this phrase implies that what the sentence was talking about wasn't revealed, when in fact it was revealed. **B is the best** choice because it agrees in number with letters and is present tense.

74) Choose the correct pronoun. Choice F is incorrect because "one" is just another way of saying you, and we're talking about Emily Dickinson. Answer G is also wrong because "people's" is not referring to Emily. And J is wrong because "their", once again, is not talking about Emily. **H is the best** answer because "her" is the best pronoun to use when talking about Emily, since it actually refers to her.

75) Comma usage is being tested here. Choice A is wrong because no comma is necessary after "legacy of letters", nor after "perhaps". Choice B is also incorrect because no commas are necessary after "this" and "letters". C is wrong because once again, no comma is necessary after "letters". In fact, no commas are needed whatsoever in this phrase, and **D** has none, deeming it **the correct** answer.

ACT MATH CONCEPTS
By **Rajiv Raju**

A comprehensive review of the mathematical concepts needed for the ACT is beyond the scope of this book. The vast majority of the questions only require middle school math, Algebra I and Geometry. There are some questions that deal with more advanced Algebra II concepts. Trigonometry is tested but there are no more than 4 questions on a typical test. At least two of these questions only deal with simple right triangle ratios and can be answered if you know the definitions of the trigonometric ratios. Advanced knowledge of trigonometry is not necessary to get a good math score.

In general, on the ACT Math section, when advanced concepts are tested they are often tested in simple straight forward questions. Do not underestimate the importance of basic concepts and skills, which are often tested in more unusual ways.

The brief listing below is intended to emphasize the most important topics that are tested and to direct the reader to real ACT questions that test the concept. The list also includes formulas that you should know. It is very important to see how the concepts are tested on real test questions because the ACT places great emphasis on the application of concepts rather than rote memorization. **The most effective way to prepare for the ACT math is to practice and analyze as many _real_ test questions as possible.**

The practice test in the booklet is only a start. You should also analyze the two additional real practice tests that are available free. For detailed instructions about how to get these free tests, see the second chapter in this book. Although the ACT test will have different questions each time, the same concepts and thinking skills tend to be tested repeatedly. By studying the three tests, you will learn the most important skills and concepts need to do well on the test. As you practice, try to come up with your own strategies to improve speed and accuracy.

Even when students understand the concepts, they often get the wrong answer because of carelessness. Common sources of error on the ACT math include not reading the question carefully and trying to solve the problem mentally instead of writing out the calculation or drawing a diagram. The more information you put down on paper, the more likely you are not to make an error.

Comparison with the SAT Math

The knowledge and skills tested on the SAT and ACT are similar, but there are also substantial differences. All of the math knowledge tested on the SAT is also tested on the ACT, but the ACT also tests additional topics not tested on the SAT. These additional topics include Trigonometry, Logarithms and Conic Sections. A typical test will have 4 trigonometry questions, one or no logarithm questions, and one or no conic section questions. If Logarithm and Conics questions are on the test, they will usually be quite basic. The questions on the ACT also tend to be more straightforward then the SAT, but the ACT gives you less time to do the questions.

Unlike the SAT math test, ACT math test often lists answer choices only in radical and fractional form. In these cases you should not do the whole problem on the calculator, since your calculator will give a decimal answer which will not match up with the answer choices.

See: Questions 14 and 12

Also unlike the SAT, there is no list of formulas at the beginning of the test. The ACT expects you to know the most important formulas such as, area formulas for circles, triangles and quadrilaterals. The listing below includes the formulas that you are expected to memorize. Less important formulas (like volume of a cylinder) are usually provided with the question.

See: Questions 29 and 30

On the SAT math the easy questions come first and the hard questions come last. This is not the case on the ACT math where there is no order of difficulty. You should never waste time on an ACT question that you are having trouble with. Just guess and go to the next question. Otherwise you may not have the opportunity to answer easy questions that may come later in the test. The ACT math test also gives you less time per question than the SAT. The ACT gives 60 seconds per math question, while the SAT gives you 75 seconds per math question. You should also be aware that the **TI-89 calculator**, which is permitted on the SAT, is **not permitted on the ACT**.

Pre-Algebra/Basic Math

Basic arithmetic is usually not directly tested. But many word problems only require translation of the problem to a basic arithmetic calculation. Almost a quarter of the test is devoted to pre algebra and basic math. Do not take these questions lightly, since it is possible to make difficult questions from simple concepts.

Some questions will test your understanding of basic math vocabulary. You should have a clear understanding of words like **factor, multiple, integer, real number,** etc.

Be careful to note subtle differences between words like positive (does not include 0) and non negative (includes 0).

See: Questions 5, 20, 47 and 48

Tables or graphs of information and numbers will be provided and you will be expected to answer questions based on the information in the table or graph. These questions usually do not require advanced mathematical concepts, but only require careful interpretation of tables or graphs and performing basic arithmetic calculations.

See: Questions 21, 28 and 34

Order of Operations

You should be familiar with how to enter expressions into your calculator so that the operations are performed in the correct order.

See: Question 2

It helps to memorize the squares and cubes of the first few numbers. This will make answering some questions much faster and easier. For example, if you see $x^3=64$ on the test you should know x=4 without having to reach for the calculator.

Squares: $2^2=4$, $3^2=9$, $4^2=16$, $5^2=25$, $6^2=36$, $7^2=49$, $8^2=64$, $9^2=81$, $10^2=100$, $11^2=124$, $12^2=144$

Cubes: $2^3=8$, $3^3=27$, $4^3=64$, $5^3=125$, $6^3=216$

Fraction, Decimal, Percent and Ratio Arithmetic

You should be able to add, subtract, multiply, divide and convert fraction and decimal percent quantities as well as deal with ratios. Questions containing these concepts are usually word problems.

Average Problems

The average of n numbers is the sum of all of these numbers dived by n. If you know the average of a set of n numbers, you usually do not know what the individual numbers are, but you can determine what the sum of all the numbers in the set is. Sum of all n numbers in the set = n x average. Calculating the sum of all the numbers is often a good way to attack ACT average problems.

See: Question 7

Do not fall for the weighted average trap. If there are 10 girls and 15 boys in a class, and the average for the girls on a test is 90 and the average for the boys is 80, what is the average score for the whole class? If you said 85 you fell for the trap! If you used the method suggested in the previous paragraph you would get the correct answer of 84. Total of scores for girls is 10x90=900. The total of scores for boys is15x 80=1200. Total of scores for class = 900+1200=2100. Average for whole class of 25 students is 2100/25=84.

Simple Descriptive Statistics

You should understand the concepts of **mean** (average), **mode** (most common) and **median** (middle value).

Distance and Time Problems

You should know how to use the formula that relates time, distance and speed. On the ACT these are usually word problems.

Distance =Speed x Time

See: Question 19

Simple Probability

These will often be word problems.

Probability=(number of favorable outcomes)/(total number of outcomes).

See: Question 24

Counting

To calculate the total number of ways things can be combined you simply multiply the number of possible choices for each category.

Example: If you have 3 types of shoes, 5 types of shirts, and 7 types of pants. The total number of ways that you

can combine these is 3x5x7=105

Elementary Algebra

Distributive property: a (b+c-d) =ab+ac-ad

See: Questions 6

Solving for one Variable in one Equation

See: Question 13

You may be given one equation with two variables and asked to solve for one of the variables in terms of the other.

You may be given an equation with two variables and asked to determine the value of an expression with those two variables. In these questions you should not try to solve for one variable. You should manipulate the equation so one side of the equation looks like the expression that they ask you to evaluate. Example: a=b+10 what does 2(a-b) equal? a-b=10 so 2(a-b)=20. Though manipulations such as these may require some algebraic insight, practicing the manipulation method on several *real* ACT problems of this nature will make them a piece of cake.

Using a Given Formula

Some questions will give you a formula and ask you to answer a question that uses the formula. Make sure you perform the calculations using the correct order of operations and make sure you use the correct units.

See: Question 33

Some questions may require you to perform simple algebraic manipulations on a given a formula.

You will be expected to translate a verbal description to an algebraic expression.

See: Questions 1, 8 and 17

Rationalizing the denominator

ACT often lists the answers in radical form with a rationalized denominator. You should know that:

$$\frac{1}{\sqrt{x}} = \frac{\sqrt{x}}{x}$$

(For those of you who didn't know, you get the expression on the right by multiplying the numerator and denominator by √X to get rid of the square root in the denominator)

Intermediate Algebra

You should memorize the equations for difference of squares and perfect square binomial

$A^2-B^2 = (A-B)(A+B)$
$(A + B)^2 = A^2 + 2AB + B^2$
$(A- B)^2 = A^2 - 2AB + B^2$

See: Question 11

Factoring quadratic equations may be needed to simplify expressions by canceling the common factors. Usually the factoring will not be very difficult.

See: Questions 23 and 38

Solving quadratic equations by factoring. Usually the factoring will not be difficult. Set each factor equal to zero and solve.

You should be familiar with **function notation** and be able to evaluate functions. If $f(x) = x^2$ then $f(-3)=9$.

See: Questions 53 and 59

You should be able make **composite functions**. If $f(x)=x^2$ and $g(x)=3x+2$ what is $f(g(x))$?

$f(g(x))=f(3x+2)= (3x+2)^2$

See: Questions 57

Absolute Value

The concept of absolute value often tested. In these cases always test your answer in the question to make sure that you did not make an error.

See: Questions 22 and 42

Inequalities

You will be expected to perform basic algebraic manipulations on inequalities.

See: Question 36

You should also be able to graph inequalities.

See: Question 49

Properties of exponents

Remember that these rules only work for the terms of the same base.

$(x^n)(x^m)=x^{(n+m)}$
$(x^n)/(x^m)=x^{(n-m)}$
$(x^n)^m=x^{nm}$

See: Question 4

Matrices

Sometimes the ACT may have one matrix question. They usually involve very simple matrix operations. Adding and subtracting matrices involves just adding or subtracting the corresponding elements in the matrix. Multiplication of very simple matrices may occasionally show up on the ACT.

Logarithms

ACT occasionally tests this concept. Logarithmic notation is just a different way to express exponents. If you are more familiar with exponents then you may want to convert the problem to exponent notation.

$$\log_b A = E \quad \text{is the same thing as} \quad b^E = A$$

See: Question 60

Coordinate Geometry

Quadrant 1: value of x and y coordinates is positive

Quadrant 2: value of x is negative and values of y is positive

Quadrant 3: value of x and y coordinates is negative

Quadrant 4: value of x coordinates is positive and value of y coordinate is negative.

Given two points (x_1,y_1) and (x_2,y_2) you should be able to calculate the slope of the line.

$$slope = \frac{y_2 - y_1}{x_2 - x_1}$$

See: Questions 12 and 43

You should be able to use the **slope intercept form** of an equation in two variables.

Y=mX + b   m=slope, b= Y intercept

See: Questions 26 and 40

You may be given equations for two lines and asked the coordinates of where they intersect. It may be faster to plug in the answers into both of the equations to see which answer works.

You are expected to know and use the **mid point formula**. An easy way to remember the formula is to see that coordinates of the midpoint are the average of coordinates of two points.

Given two points (x_1, y_1) and (x_2, y_2) the midpoint (x_m, y_m) is:

$$x_m = \frac{x_1 + x_2}{2}$$

$$y_m = \frac{y_1 + y_2}{2}$$

You should know the **distance formula**. The distance between two points $(x_1, y1)$ and $(x_2, y2)$ is:

$$D = \sqrt{(x_2 - x_1)^2 + (y_2 - y_1)^2}$$

The ACT has an occasional question about parabolas, circles and ellipses. These only require a very basic understanding of the equations for these relations.

A **parabola** opening upward with vertex at origin:

$y = x^2$

See: Question 50

A **circle** with radius **r** and center **(h,k)** :

$(x-h)^2+(y-k)^2=r^2$

An **ellipse** with center (h,k) , horizontal axis 2a and vertical axis 2b

$$\frac{(x-h)^2}{a^2} + \frac{(y-k)^2}{b^2} = 1$$

Sequences

Arithmetic Sequences- each pair of successive terms differs by the same amount.

Example: 1, 5, 10,15, 20, 25, 30.... a difference between successive terms of 5

Most sequence questions can be answered by writing out about 5 terms and looking for a pattern. The question may be in to form of a word problem. Usually, if there are a manageable number of terms, it is to your advantage to write out the sequence. Don't trust just your brain's ability to visualize patterns, trust your brain and your eyes! As Albert Einstein so eloquently stated: "The pencil adds 30 points to your IQ.." Use your pencil, especially for these types of problems!

See: Question 3

Plane Geometry

Distance between points on a line. You may be given multiple points
on a line segment along with the distance between some of these
points. You may be asked to figure out the distance between a set of
points. Example:

A   B C   D

.   . .   .

AD=30 and AC=16 what is BC?

In problems like this, it is very useful to label the given distances on
the picture.

Angles

You should be abele to find angles based on given information. Listed
below are come common geometric properties that are useful for
finding angles on the ACT.

-Adjacent angles that form straight line will add up to 180.

-Angles of a triangle add up to 180

-Vertical angles are congruent.

*-Corresponding angels and alternate interior angles formed by
transversals and parallel lines are congruent.*

*-Corresponding angles of similar and congruent triangles are
congruent.*

See: Questions 18, 39 and 45

Triangles

Triangles Properties are tested quite often. If you have had geometry they should not be difficult. The special propertied of **Isosceles, equilateral and right triangles** are especially popular on the test.

See: Questions16, 44 and 45

You should know the formula **for area of triangle.**

A= (1/2)bh where b=base and h=height

Pythagorean Theorem

Leg1^2 + Leg2^2 = Hypotenuse^2

Questions that use the Pythagorean Theorem are on every ACT. To decrease the chance of error and increase speed, it may be a good idea "pre solve" this equation for the hypotenuse and each of the legs. This way you will not make common mistakes like forgetting to take the square root to find the length of a side. When asked to calculate the leg or hypotenuse you can use these two forms of this equation.

$$leg_1 = \sqrt{hyp^2 - leg_2^2}$$
$$hyp = \sqrt{leg_1^2 + leg_2^2}$$

It is worth memorizing these two Pythagorean triples because they save you time and decrease chance of error.

3 : 4 : 5

5 : 12 : 13

You should also know the ratios for sides of the 45-90-45 and 30-60-90 right triangles.

45-90-45 : $1 : \sqrt{2} : 1$

30-60-90 : $1 : \sqrt{3} : 2$

Some word problems require the use of the Pythagorean Theorem.

See: Questions 14 and 35

You should be able to calculate **perimeter and area** of common objects. Some questions require you to translate words to a figure and then calculate.

Perimeter of rectangle= 2 (length + width)

Parallelograms

You will be expected to know the formula for the **area of a parallelogram**.

A=bh; where b=base and h=height

Areas of other polygons

On the ACT you can usually find areas of other polygons like trapezoids by adding area of rectangles and triangles.

It is worth memorizing the formula for the sum of the interior angles of a convex polygon.

Sum of interior angles of polygon of n sides = (n-2)x180

See: Question 45

Circle Properties

You are expected to know formulas for area and circumference.

$$A = \pi r^2$$

$$C = 2\pi r$$

See: Question 54

You will need to determine measurements for parts of circle. For example if the circumference of an entire circle is 100 then the length of a 60 degree sector is (60/360)x100=16.667.

See: Question 30

A radius drawn to the point of tangency is perpendicular to the tangent.

A radius drawn perpendicular to a chord always bisects the chord.

Solid Geometry

Some questions dealing with solid objects will give you the needed formula, but you will be expected to know simple formulas such as the volume a box= length x width x height.

You should also be able to calculate areas of boxes. Formulas for things like volumes of cylinders are usually given in the problem. It is not necessary to memorize obscure solid geometry formulas, but if you are given a formula you should be able to use it to answer the question.

See: Question 29 and 46

Trigonometry

There are no more that 4 trigonometry questions on a typical ACT test. Most of these do not need advanced knowledge. If you learn the definitions given below and learn how to use them, you have good chance of correctly answering two or three of these questions.

$$\sin\theta = \frac{opposite\_side}{hypotenuse}$$

$$\cos\theta = \frac{adjacent\_side}{hypotenuse}$$

$$\tan\theta = \frac{opposite\_side}{adjacent\_side}$$

$$\csc\theta = \frac{hypotenuse}{opposite} = \frac{1}{\sin\theta}$$

$$\sec\theta = \frac{hypotenuse}{adjacent} = \frac{1}{\cos\theta}$$

See: Questions 25 and 32

Also worth memorizing is:

$$\tan\theta = \frac{\sin\theta}{\cos\theta}$$

Notice that **if you know any two of these ratios, you can figure out all five of the ratios.**

The **Pythagorean identity** is worth memorizing for the ACT.

$$(\sin x)^2 + (\cos x)^2 = 1$$

Solve this for sin x and cos x to get:

$$\sin x = \sqrt{1-(\cos x)^2}$$
$$\cos x = \sqrt{1-(\sin x)^2}$$

When ever you see Sin(x)^2 + Cos(x)^2, you can replace it by 1 to simplify the expression.

Also if you see $\sqrt{1-(\cos x)^2}$ you can replace it by Sin(x).

Similarly $\sqrt{1-(\sin x)^2}$ can be replaced by Cos(x).

You are not expected to memorize a large number of obscure trigonometric identities, but you may be given an identity and asked to use it to answer the question. These questions can be answered by applying the rules of algebra to the given identity.

Graphs of trigonometric functions

The ACT sometimes has one question dealing with graphs of trigonometric functions. These usually deal with how parts of the functions change the amplitude and period of the graph. If you have had trigonometry in school these questions should not be too difficult. If you have not had a trigonometry class, just guess and go on to the next question.

Miscellaneous questions

Some questions just require careful reading and thinking.

See: Questions 15, 51 and 52

Translating verbal descriptions to graphs

See: Question 31

Logic Questions

These are perhaps the most obscure questions on the test. They usually will be something along the lines of this:

"If 1 is true, then 2 is true; Which of the following is true?"

For these types of questions, simple reasoning should be applied.

The only answer that makes sense is "If 1 is not true, then 2 is not true", since 2's truth is dependent on 1's truth. Don't let these questions catch you off guard. All they require is a little common sense.

ACT MATH TEST EXPLANATIONS
By **Rajiv Raju**

Please refer to the questions in the Math component of the practice test in official ACT booklet, <u>Preparing for the ACT</u> (2008/2009).

1) When faced with word problems that involve translating dissipations to mathematical expressions, first identify the constant and variable components and be careful not to mix-up these components. The most common mix-ups will be listed as wrong answer choices. The first thing you should do is to see what is constant and what varies. In this problem, the base price, or the cost of the machine, $39.99, is the constant. The cost to make each balloon, $2.00 a piece, is the element in the equation that varies. "*b*" is the variable for the number of balloons. We now have everything necessary to form our expression in this case:

$$\$2.00b+\$39.99$$

This happens to be answer **choice A** on the test. This expression has the correct variable ($2.00b) and constant ($39.99) terms. Three of the wrong answers do not have a constant term. Choices B, D, and E, are wrong because they have no constant in the expression and two of the choices have random values that are not given in the problem. Choice C is wrong because the value that is supposed to be constant (39.99) is placed in front of b and is varied, while the value that is supposed to vary (2.00) is made constant.

An alternative approach to this problem involves trying easy numbers and testing the answer choices. What is the total cost to produce 3 balloons? From reading the problem we can calculate this cost to be $45.99. Testing the answer choices we see that A is the only answer that gives this value. If you choose to use this approach do not start with numbers like 0, 1 or 2 which will often work for some of the wrong answers. If the number you pick works for more than one answer choice then you have test more numbers until you can find the one correct choice. In this case if you tested b=1 it would work for both A, C and D. Trying numbers is probably not worth the time if you can figure out how to translate the word problem to a mathematical expression. However, this approach is helpful if you are not sure how to do the problem using the usual method.

2) This problem is very simple and there is no other way to do it other than plugging in the values for the variables and following the order of operations and rules of addition and subtraction. Since this is a very simple problem, it should be very quick and the other answers are wrong because they are computation errors you can make while evaluating the values for x and y. If you were careful then you should get the correct answer 36 or **choice K**. If made an error you should identify your error so that you can try to avoid it in the future. If you picked H you probably carelessly subtracted 1 form 5 instead of adding.

3) This problem might seem very tedious at first, but there is an easier way to do it. Since the teacher taught the students 5 words on the first day and 3 words each day after that for 19 more days, we can just multiply 3 and 19 and add 5:

(3 x 19)+ 5=62

This is the number of words that the students learn in 20 days, and this happens to be **choice B**. When ever you are given these types of number problems, another way to find the answer quickly is to write out the values for the first few days and see if there is a pattern.(Remember that quote by Albert Einstine) Actually writing out some numbers will help you see the pattern. If you familiar with arithmetic series from your math classes, you may see that this question deals with that concept. However, you can still answer this question correctly even if you are not familiar with this concept by using the common sense approach.

4) This problem tests your ability to correctly use the rules of exponents to simplify the expression. When doing this problem, you should make sure to follow the rules of exponents while raising the powers of the values in the parenthesis. If you simplify correctly, you should get- $64x^6$ or **choice G**. Choice F has the correct coefficient, but a wrong exponent for x. Choice H doesn't follow the rules of exponents, and the 4 is multiplied by3 in stead of being raised to the

third power, even though the exponent on x is correct. Choice J makes this same error, and the exponent on x is incorrect, because 3 is added to 2 instead of multiplied, which is the rule when raising an exponent to a certain power. Choice K completely ignores 4 and only raises the exponent of x to the third power. When you are raising a value in parenthesis to a certain power, make sure you raise all of the terms in the parenthesis.

5) This problem asks you to find all of the positive factors of 8, which is one of the easiest problems you will come across. First you must know what a factor is. A factor is a number that multiplies into a larger number evenly. If you do not know all of the factors of 8 off the top of your head, you can try every number from 1 through 8. The obvious values are one and 8 and if the answers don't have these values, you can eliminate them, so you can eliminate B and C. If you find the other factors, they are 1, 2, 4, 8, which **happens to be E**. Answer A is wrong because it does not include 2 and 4, and answer D is wrong because 16 and 32 are not even factors, but they are multiples.

6) To do this problem, we need to combine all the like terms. Follow the order of operations to do this and multiply out the parenthesis getting:

8x+14-6x+12

Then you combine the x's and the integers to get 2x+26, which is **choice H**. Answer F is wrong because it has a random x value and has 2 as the integer. This mistake can be made when you forget that the answer is positive when you multiply -3 and -4. In G, this same mistake is made even when the x value is correct. Answer J is wrong just because it has random values for x and the constant. This is also true for K.

7) This is a very easy problem. All you have to do is drop the lowest score and then take the average of the remaining numbers: 78, 83, 84, 93. The average of this 84.5 which is **answer E**. Choice B is wrong because you get that answer if you forget to drop the lowest score. Choice A is wrong even though it drops the lowest score because it still divides the answer by 5 instead of changing it to 4 because there are only 4 values.

8) Notice that the answers are in increasing order. If we want to try out the choices to see which answer will work, the easiest way to do this problem is to start with the middle choice H and go from there, but first you have to set up equations for each cable provider. For the first one, Uptown, you try to find the terms that vary and the terms that are constant. The term that varies is the $25 a month charge and the constant is the one time $120 setup fee. For Downtown, the constant is the $60 one time set up charge and the thing that varies is the $35 a month charge. If we let x be time in months, our 2 expressions:

Cost for Uptown =25x+120

Cost for Downtown=35x+60

Now we start testing the answers with choice H. Since Uptown costs more for choice C, 10 months, we can eliminate J and K, now we try choice G. This choice happens to make the price of the two providers equal, so **choice G** ,6, is the answer. Since we have already found the answer to the problem we do not need to try F.

An alternative approach is to realize that when the costs of the two cable providers are equal the equation is true:

25x+120=35x+60

If you solve for x you get the correct answer 6.

9) Although this problem looks very tedious, it is not. The key phrase in the problem is "adjacent sides meet at right angles". This lets you conclude that opposite sides are parallel. Since the sides opposite the sides with unknown values are given, we can just assume that all of the unknown sides add up to the side opposite them. All you have to do now is calculate the perimeter as you would in a square for this particular problem. Since the sides opposite the unknown sides are both 20 each, we can conclude that the sum of the unknown vertical and horizontal sides each add up to 20. We just add them up and we get 80 or **choice B**. This is really the only choice that can be reasonably derived from the information given.

10) The easiest way to solve this problem is to set up 2 equations:

x+y=11

x-y=5

If you add the two equations together, you get 2x=16 because the y variables cancel out. This becomes x=8, and you plug this into the first equation to get 3 for y, and you multiply these to get 24, which is **choice J**. Some possible traps are answer choices F, H, and K. In F, the answer is only the y value, not xy. In H the answer is the x value, not xy. In K the value is multiplying the difference, 5 by the sum, 11, which is completely incorrect. Wrong answers often will be numbers that you may get while doing the problem, but are not what they are asking for. Make sure that you are actually answering the question.

11) You should memorize the formulas for perfect square binomials. In this problem we would use the formula:

$(a+b)^2 = a^2+2ab+b^2$

If we apply this for the given expression and we get $9x^2+42x+49$, which is answer **choice E**. Choice A is wrong because it only multiplies each term in the parenthesis by 2 instead of squaring it. Choice B is wrong because although it squares x, the coefficients and constants are still only multiplied by 2. Choice C is wrong because, it does not follow the special case and forgets about the 2ab. Choice D is wrong because it only multiplies ab instead of 2ab in the expression. If you forget the formula, you can still do the problem by using FOIL on (a+b) (a+b), but you can answer the questing much faster and with less chance of error if you know the formula.

12) This is a simple problem of calculating the slope given 2 points. The formula for the slope is:

Slope= change in y / change in x:

$$slope = \frac{y_2 - y_1}{x_2 - x_1}$$

If we plug our points in to the formula we get:

$$slope = \frac{2-7}{-5-6} = \frac{5}{11}$$

This turns out to be 5/11, which is answer **choice J**. Answer choice F is wrong because it just adds the two y values. Answer choice G is wrong because it just subtracts the 2 y values. Answer H also subtracts the 2 y values only. K does not follow the rules of division and keeps – (5/11) instead of 5/11 because it disregards that 2 negatives make a positive when dividing or multiplying. If you are a calculator wiz and have a program on your calculator to calculate slope, you will not find your decimal answer in the choices and will have to figure out which answer choice corresponds to your answer. This is another example when calculator overuse can make the problem more complicated.

13) The simplest way to do this problem is to solve the equation. There are multiple ways to do this, but only one will be discussed here. First, you multiply each term by 3, to get rid of 1/3x, then 4, until you get this:

4k+3k=12

Then you combine the k terms to get: 7k = 12, then you divide and get k = 12/7, which is answer **choice B**. This is the only reasonable answer that can be derived from manipulation.

14) If you know the Pythagorean theorem, this is an extremely simple problem. For right triangles:

$$hypotenuse^2 = leg1^2 + leg2^2$$

$$hypotenuse = \sqrt{(leg1^2 + leg2^2)}$$

In our case leg1=6 and leg2=7:

$$hypotenuse = \sqrt{6^2 + 7^2} = \sqrt{85}$$

The correct answer is **choice G.**

The ACT often gives answers in radical and fractional form. If you had done the whole calculation on calculator without looking at the answers, you would waste time and increase chance of error by trying to figure out which answer choice matches your decimal calculator answer. Use the calculator only when you need it. On the ACT some times the calculator actually slows you down.

Choice F is wrong because it is just adding the 2 values and taking the square root of the sum. Choice H does this also except it doesn't take the square root. Choice K just multiplies the 2 side lengths, which does not help you find the hypotenuse.

15) The simplest way to do this problem is to add up the squares and the square fractions. There are 18 full squares and 4 fractional squares. You can estimate the sum of the square fractions to be 2 full squares. Match up all of the like squares and fractions and add them all together and you get 20, or **choice C**. A potential source of error is not adding the fractions correctly or disregarding the fractions all together.

16) This question tests your knowledge of geometry. We are given enough information to conclude that triangles ADB and BCA are congruent right triangles using the HL theorem for right

triangles. We are given that one leg is congruent. The hypotenuse is shared. We have to look at the answers and decide which one cannot be reasonably inferred from the given information. All of the choices except G are corresponding parts of the two congruent triangles. G cannot be determined because there are no sides or angles that can be used to determine their congruence. **G is the correct answer.** Choice F is wrong because it can be inferred because they represent corresponding parts of congruent triangles. Choice H is wrong for the same reason except these are segments of the longer sides. J is wrong because corresponding angles in congruent triangles are congruent. Choice K is wrong for the same reason.

17) For this problem we have to set up an expression to describe the situation. Since it is talking about 23%, we have to convert this to .23 for the problem. Since p is the price and 0.23p is the amount of discount. p-0.23p is the discounted price. This is **choice A.** Choice B is wrong because if forgets the p after 0.23. Choice C is wrong because it has 23 instead of 0.23. D is wrong because it does not have 0.23p or the decimal in front of 23. E is wrong because it only shows the discount, not the <u>discounted price.</u>

18) To do this problem we need an understanding of triangles and their angles. First, you should write down your given information in the designated areas: 76 degrees, 47 degrees, 140 degrees. Since we know that the sum 2 angles that form a line is 180 degrees, CBD is 40 degrees. Now that we have that info and 47 degrees, we find that CDB is 93 degrees. From that, we find that CDA is 87 degrees. If we add the measures CAD and CDA, we get 163 degrees. Since there are 180 degrees in a triangle, we subtract:

180-163=17, which is **answer H.**

19) To do this problem, we need to know the formula: D=RT, which is *distance equals rate times time.* First, we need to find the time it takes to drive with the given info. By plugging in 900 and 50 for D and R respectively and solving, we get T=18 hours. The problem asks how much the average speed is for this time-3, which is 15. Now we set up our equation again except now we solve for R and plug 15 hours into T. Solving, we get 60 mph. We must subtract the original speed to get the speed increase, or how much Ms. Lewis needs to increase her

average speed. The answer is 10, which is **choice C**. A possible trap is choice E because that is the only the answer for the number of hours of driving, not the question. Choice D is also a trap because that is just the time it take after subtracting 3 from 18.

20) The simple way to attack this problem is to try the answer choices. First, see if all the answer choices divide evenly into both numbers. This is easy because you have a calculator. You find that G does not plug into 180x evenly, so you can eliminate that since the answers with x in them are going to be the greatest answers out of the remaining because in this question x can only be a positive integer, you can also eliminate F. Now, you just pick answer with the largest coefficient, 36x is the answer, which is answer **choice K**.

21) If you look at the table you should see that the larger bags give you the lowest cost per lemon. To get the lowest cost we want to get as many large bags as possible without going over 20. We can only get one bag of 12 and one bag of 6 without exceeding 20. 12+6=18 so we need to get two bags of one to get exactly twenty. If we add up the cost of one bag of 12, one bag of 6 and two bags of 1 you get the lowest cost to get 20 lemons which is $3.90 or **B**. Some of the other answer choices also give the cost of 20 lemons but they do not give us the lowest cost to get exactly 20.

22) This problem tests your understanding of absolute value. Since it is asking for the maximum diameter that satisfies the inequality:

$$|d-3| \leq 0.001$$

Choices H, J and K satisfy the inequality but **only K** gives the maximum diameter. The other choices do not satisfy the given inequality.

23) For this problem, the easiest thing to do is to just factor the expression and see which answer corresponds to your answer. If you factor like you were thought in your math class you will get (5x+2)(x-3), which is **choice A**. All of the other choices either mix up

the signs of the numbers or interchange the integers 3 and 2 in the factors. If you have trouble factoring you can try the answers until find the correct one, but factoring will be faster.

24) The easiest way to do this problem is to plug in answers and see which one will cause the answer to yield 3/5. You need to add red marbles until the probability of picking a red marble is 3/5. To start, you try out H. Because the answer is greater than 3/5, you can eliminate J and K. If you try G it is still greater than 3/5. If you **try F**, you get 18 out of 30 marbles are red, which is 3/5, which is the answer.

25) If you know the definitions of trigonometric ratios, this problem will take 5 seconds. For any acute angle θ in a right triangle:

$$\sin \theta = \frac{opposite}{hypotenuse}$$

We are told that the triangle is formed by a diagonal in a rectangle. So we can infer that the triangle is right. For angle w the opposite side is x and the hypotenuse is y. Since all the answer choices have the ratio (x/y) in them, we know the answer has to have sin in it because opposite/hypotenuse(x/y) is equal to sine. The only **answer choice** in it with sine **is D**. All other choices are wrong because they show incorrect rules for all the other trig ratios. Even if you have not had a course in trigonometry is worth memorizing the trigonometric ratios since they are tested on every ACT test.

26) When you given an equation for a line in the y=mx+b form the slope is m. We are given two equations in this form. Therefore, if the slope is larger, the "m" is larger. So if the first equation has more slope, then a>c is the only possible answer, which is **answer J**.

27) There are six nails. From any nail you can stretch five rubber bands to the other nails. If you did this at each nail you would have placed 5 x 6 = 30 rubber bands, but you would have placed two rubber bands between each pair of nails. The total number of ways to stretch one rubber band all the nails is half this number which is 15 or **choice A**.

Another way to approach the problem is to draw all the possible lines and count them. If you try this approach you have to have an organized way to draw all lines without duplication.

28) To do this problem, add up all the participants to get 280. Divide the number of runners aged 26-35 the total to get 112/280 to get 0.4. Now you just multiply .4 by 60 to get your answer, 24, or **choice H**. This is the simplest way to do it, although you could set up a proportion:

112/280=x/60

and then solve for x. This would take a little more time to solve, however, and your aim is to take the least time possible on each question while still remaining accurate.

29)   To do this problem, all you have to do is apply the given formula for the volume of the cylinder to find the volume of water. Remember you were asked to find the volume of water, not the pool. We have to use a height of 5 ft   First, you interpret the given information to find your radius, 12 ft, and your height, 5 ft.

$$volume = \pi r^2 h = \pi 12^2 5 = 2262$$

 When you use this formula you get volume of 2262 which is the answer, rounded to the nearest cubic foot. This happens to be **choice C**. Be sure not to waste your time on unnecessary information, like the degree measure, 75, that is given in the problem.   This is irrelevant to finding the volume of the cylinder.

30) This problem requires you to find the circumference of the pool, and then solve the rest of the problem from there. The formula for circumference of a circle with radius r is:

$$circumference = 2\pi r = 2\pi 12 = 24\pi = 75.4$$

Using an r of 12 we get a circumference of 75.4. Since you are given the degree measure of the arc, you just divide that measure by the total degree measure of a circle to find the fraction of the circle that makes up the arc:

45/360= 0.125

After this, you can multiply that fraction (or decimal) by the circumference of the pool to find the measure of the outer arc: 9 .425.

0.125 x 75.4 = 9.425

But that is not the whole problem. You must also add the radius, which is 12 feet. If you add these two values, you get 21.425.

9.425+ 12 = 21.425

This is closest to 22 in the answer choices, which **happens to be G**. Some potential errors are finding the area instead of the circumference, or not adding the radius length after finding the outer arc length.

31) To do this problem, you need to know how to translate this problem into a graph representing it. Since the pool is increasing the whole time, and the rate of increase slows after the larger flow hose stops, the graph will decrease in slope at a certain point after the beginning. The only graph that represents this is **graph E**. Graph A is wrong because it shows a smaller slope then a larger slope. Graph B is wrong because it has a decreasing graph. Graph C is wrong because it is constantly increasing. Graph D is wrong because it is also decreasing.

32) To solve this problem, you need to set up an equation with the trigonometric ratio for tangent. For an acute angle θ in a right triangle:

$$\tan\theta = \frac{opposite}{adjacent}$$

For this problem x is the unknown adjacent side we are trying to determine:

$$\tan 75 = \frac{6}{x}$$

Solving for x:

$$x = \frac{6}{\tan 75}$$

which is answer **choice F**. A possible trap is J because it messes up the ratio by using adjacent/ opposite, resulting in x/6=tan 75, which yields 6 tan 75.

33) This problem is very easy because all you have to do is set it up. Plug in the variables and you have the answer. If you plug in 5%, you get 5/100, which is .05. Plug in 782,000 for P_o and 10 years(2000-1990) and you get $782,000(1.05)^{10}$, which is **choice C**. Be careful not to be tricked by other answers. For example, E puts 782000 into the parenthesis, when it is supposed to be kept outside, as stated in the formula.

34) To do this problem, you should first go down the chart and group each call into its respective pricing and then go from there. Then you should multiply the prices by the number of minutes in each part of the chart and add all the charges up. If you do your addition correctly, you should get $8.80, which **is choice J**. Be sure not to get the PM times mixed up with the 7:00 pm-7:00 am .10 cent period.

35) For this problem, you have to use the properties of trapezoids and the Pythagorean theorem to solve the problem. First, since the trapezoid is and isosceles trapezoid, you can draw heights on either side of the smaller parallel side inside the trapezoid. Since the smaller side is 10 and the larger side is 16, and this is an isosceles

trapezoid, you can divide the remaining length 6 in half, giving you one of your sides in a right triangle. Since the hypotenuse is 5, and the known side of the triangle is 3, the other leg must be 4. This is also the height and answer **choice B**. The ACT often uses Pythagorean triples. This is a 3,4,5 triple. Knowing these Pythagorean triples increases your speed and accuracy.

36) This is a very straight-forward problem. All you have to do is solve for x in the inequality.

3(x+2) > 4(x-3)

3x+6 > 4x-12

x > 18

First, you have to distribute out the expressions on each side of the inequality. There are many ways you can manipulate this problem, but the quickest is to move the 3x to the right and the -12 to the left, resulting in:

18>x, or in proper terms, x<18

This is answer **choice K**. If you don't mess up the manipulations and follow all the steps just as you would a normal equation with the few exceptions in inequalities, this is one of the easiest problems you will encounter on this test.

37) For this problem, you need to have an understanding of the midpoint formula.

Given two points (x_1,y_1) and (x_2,y_2) the midpoint (x_m,y_m) is:

$$x_m = \frac{x_1+x_2}{2} = \frac{1+x}{2} = 4$$

$$y_m = \frac{y_1+y_2}{2} = \frac{-5+y}{2} = -3$$

Using this formula we get 4=(1+x)/2 and -3=(-5+y)/2. Solving for x we get x=7. Solving for y we get y=-1. x+y=6 or **C**.

38) To do this problem, you need to know how to factor out terms from an expression. It is worth memorizing the difference of squares formula:

$a^2-b^2=(a-b)(a+b)$

$$\frac{x+1}{x(x^2-1)} = \frac{x+1}{x(x+1)(x-1)} = \frac{1}{x(x-1)} = \frac{1}{x^2-x}$$

If you look at the denominator of the expression, you can factor out an x right at front you are then left with $x(x^2-1)$.   You can further factor this expression (easy of you realize that you are dealing with a difference of squares) to get the following value in the denominator:

$x(x+1)(x-1)$

There is x+1 in the numerator, you can cancel out the x+1 to get x(x-1), which turns into x^2-x, with 1 in the numerator.   The final answer should look like **choice J**.

Beware of trick answers like H, which has a -1 in the denominator instead of –x.

39) You can determine angle ACB is 50 degrees because 180-130=50 since a straight line forms 180 degree and we are given the other part of the straight angle is 130. Because the sum of the angles of a triangle is 180 we can determine that angel ABC is also 50.You then proceed to fill in all the angles that are congruent to 50. If you follow these rules of congruence for vertical angles, corresponding and alternate interior angles of the transversal of parallel lines, you should find 8 angles that are congruent to 50 degrees, which is **choice C**.

40) To solve this problem, you first need to set up an equation representing the adult and student tickets and how much they all add up to.

3x+2y=600

is the equation, with x representing the adult tickets, and y representing the student tickets.   The coefficients represent their prices respectively.

If you isolate y, you get:

y= -(3/2)x+300

Since the y intercept is 300, we can eliminate all answers besides K and H. If you find the slope of each line, you find that **H** is the only one with –(3/2) as the slope. Beware not to pick the answers that have 600 as the y intercept, such as F and G. This occurs if you forget to divide the entire expression by 2 when you have 2y=-3x+600 and leave 600.

41)This is perhaps the easiest problem you can ever encounter on this test. All you need is knowledge of the elementary concept of median. This problem is made even easier because there are seven numbers. All you have to do is order them in increasing order and pick the one that is right in the middle, or the 4th number. This number is 42, which is answer **choice A**. A trick answer is choice E. Although 79 is the 4th number, this series of numbers is not ordered correctly.

42) This problem is just a factoring problem with the addition of absolute value signs. If you factor the expression: $|x|^2+2|x|-3$, you get $(|x|+3)(|x|-1)$, which leads to: $|x|=-3$ and $|x|=1$, which in turn leads to (+ or -)1 and (+ or -)3, which would appear to be the answer. But for absolute value problems, you always need to check your final answers, and if you plug all your answers in you find that + or – 1 are the only answers that work. **The answer is F.** Choice G is the opposite of the right answer, and only can occur if you check your answers wrong. Choice H is wrong because not only does it disregard the absolute value, it contains an answer that doesn't fit. Choice J also makes this error. If find factoring with absolute value confusing, just try all the answers until you find the correct one.

43)To do this problem, you need to have an understanding of the slope formula(change y/change x). Since you are given (2,5), you can see what y value you have to subtract to get 2, and this is 3. Since the only answers with 3 as the y value are A and D, you can eliminate all other answers. Now you see which value leads to - 3(since the final answer is negative), and this is 5. The only answer with these x and y values **is D**, (5,3).

44) In this figure, we are given 2 right triangles. Since we are given a 30 degree angle in one triangle and a 60 degree angle in the other, we know these are the special 30, 60, 90 degree triangles. This

establishes that the triangles are similar, and that corresponding sides will be in proportion. The long legs will be in proportion. The only ratio that is correct is **choice F**, or AB: AD. Choice G is wrong because it is comparing one of the legs of the smaller triangle to the hypotenuse of the larger triangle. H is wrong because it doesn't even compare sides of the separate triangles, but only sides in the larger triangle. Choice J is wrong because it compares the wrong legs instead of the corresponding legs. Choice K is wrong because it also compares one of the legs of the smaller triangle to the hypotenuse of the larger triangle.

45) To do this problem, you first need to know that the triangle formed is an isosceles triangle since it is extended from 2 sides in a regular pentagon, where all the sides are congruent. You now have to find the measure of all the angles in the polygon, and we can use the formula for the sum of all interior angles and divide by 5 to get the measure of one angle:

sum of interior angles of polygon of n sides=(n-2)x180

for a regular pentagon each angle is

((5-2)x180) / 5=108   ....you plug in 5 for n in the formula.

If you do this you find that the pentagon has a measure of 108 degrees for each of its angles. Now you can find the measure of the angles of the triangle, which are the same because the triangle is isosceles. The measure for both base angles is 180-108=72. Now you can find the measure of x by adding 72 and 72 together and subtracting from 180, getting 36, or **choice C**. Choice E and D are both traps. Choice E is a trap because it answers the wrong question, the measure of the base angles instead of the measure of x. Choice D is something you would get if you tried to estimate with your eyes, because it resembles a 45 degree angle.

46) To do this problem, you must NOT confuse surface area with volume. You need to know that a cube has 6 faces. From there, you just find the area of each face, 9, because the edges are 3, and multiply by 6, the number of faces, which gives you 54, **or K**. Choice H is a blatant trap because it gives the answer for volume and not surface area. Choice A is also a trap because it has the area of a square with edge 3, not a cube with edge 3.

47) This problem is very easy, but it is easy to get tricked. The easiest way to do this problem is to start with 100. You increase 100 by 25%, giving you 125. You then take 20% away from 125 you get 100 again, which happens to be **choice C**. Do not fall for choice D which incorrectly subtracts the percentages to get 105%. For these percent increase and decrease problems it is helpful to assume that you are dealing with the number 100.

48) For this problem, you need to use the definition of reciprocals. Just plug in a number for x to see which choice corresponds to that number's location on the number line. Let's try 2 for this problem. The reciprocal of 2 is ½ since 2x1/2 is 1. This is **choice J**, which states that the reciprocal is between 0 and 1. Remember that a number's reciprocal is just a fraction with the number in the denominator and 1 in the numerator. (3 the reciprocal is 1/3). Choice F is wrong because a number that is greater than 1 times its reciprocal cannot be negative. Choice G is wrong because in this choice, the answer is still negative. Choice H is wrong because the reciprocal cannot be 0 because you cannot have a real reciprocal that is 0 since 1/0 is undefined. Choice K is wrong because the reciprocal of a number greater than 1 cannot be also greater than 1. The reciprocal of this type of number is always a fraction.

49) This is a very straight-forward problem. You might be thrown off by the awkward presentation of the inequalities(-1>x instead of x<-1). Since the graph is greater from 3 onwards or is less than or equal to 1, the correct inequality **is D**. A is wrong because it says that x is greater than or equal to 1, when it is less than or equal to 1. C is wrong because in makes the same mistake in A and also mixes up the second part by saying that x is less than or equal to 3. Choice E is wrong because it states that x is less than or equal to 1 , but wrongly states that x is less than or equal to 3.

50) This problem is easy if you know how to translate the word problem into an equation. The problem seems complicated since it asks for a graph that for each y coordinate, it is 1 less than the square of the x coordinate. You can translate this into an equation, however:

$y=x^2-1$

Now this is just a simple translation problem where you have to identify the graph. Since the -1 is not in parenthesis, that means there is a vertical shift 1 unit down from the standard graph of x², a parabola. The only choice that has this **is J**. Choice F and G are wrong because they are not even parabolas. Choice H is wrong because it makes a vertical shift 1 unit upwards instead of 1 unit down. Choice K is wrong because it flips the graph over the x axis and shifts it down 1 unit, giving it the graph of: $y=-x^2-1$.

51) To be able to do this question you have to understand that they are asking for the smallest number that can be repeatedly divided evenly by 3 4 times. . Easiest way to do the problem is to try the answer choices on the calculator. Only one of the answer choices can be divided evenly by 3 repeatedly 4 times. 81/3=27, 27/3=9, 9/3=3 and 3/3=1. The correct answer is **81 or E**. If you start with the middle choice 27 or C you can save time by not having to try all of the choices. 27/3=9 and 9/3=3 and 3/1=1 so we know that 27 is too small and we do not have to try the smaller choices A and B. Now try 54 54/3=18, 18/3=6,6/3=2 but 2 is not divisible by 3 so the answer must be 81 or choice E.

52) To do this problem, you have to just plug in numbers to find which rule it satisfies. For this, it is very important to check for multiple numbers! Let's use 1 and 2. If we look at F We can see that m is odd, but if you use 2 and 3, you see this rule doesn't hold up. Choice G also is true for some cases with consecutive integers, but not when n is even. Choice H is wrong for all cases since the difference of consecutive integers is always 1. **Choice J** is the only choice that works for multiple possibilities of consecutive integers. n^2-m^2 is odd is always true for all consecutive integers. Since you have found your answer, there is no need to check K. For these types of problems, it is always good to start with the first choice and go down.

53) While this problem may seem complicated , this problem just asks you to follow the rules and evaluate the expression. Since the number you are evaluating for is less than 0, you use the second function. If you plug it in you get P(-1)=-70, or answer **choice A**. Be sure to follow the rules. A common misconception for piecewise functions is that you plug in the variable for both functions and add them. You MUST pick the function that satisfies the number being evaluated.

54) This problem tests your understanding of the formulas regarding a circle. The diameter, 3 feet, is given, and 5 inches must hang over. To do this problem, the first step must be to add the entire length of the diameter including the extra 5 inches on each side. 3 feet is 36 inches. You add 10 inches to that since the diameter is the distance between 2 sides going through the middle of the circle. This adds up to 46 inches. However, if you look at the problem, 46 inches is not an answer choice. But the problem asks which choice is the minimum needed, and **48, or K**, is the only choice that satisfies the need for 46 inches. Although these types of problems may stump you, you must always remember to read the question carefully, not missing any key points.

55) This question tests your understanding of the basic graphs of sine and cosine. However, this problem is very easy if you have had trigonometry. If you have not had trigonometry you need to learn that a_1 and a_2 determine the amplitude. Just order the graphs up in increasing amplitude. Obviously, 0 has an amplitude of 0, a_2 has the smaller visible amplitude, and a_1 has the larger visible amplitude. The answer that orders these correctly **is B**. Don't get confused by these graphs. Comparing the amplitudes is the easiest way to order the graphs with the highest values.

56) You have to know the pathogen identity to do this problem:

$$(\sin x)^2 + (\cos x)^2 = 1$$

Solve this for sin x and cos x to get:

$$\sin x = \sqrt{1 - (\cos x)^2}$$

$$\cos x = \sqrt{1 - (\sin x)^2}$$

If you substitute the above expressions into the expression in the problem you get:

$$\frac{\sqrt{1-(\cos x)^2}}{\sin x} + \frac{\sqrt{1-(\sin x)^2}}{\cos x} = \frac{\sin x}{\sin x} + \frac{\cos x}{\cos x} = 1 + 1 = 2$$

This is answer **choice H**.

57) To do this problem, you need to understand function notation and how to combine functions. You are given a point (4, 6) and 2 functions that the point passes through: $f(x)=\sqrt{x}$ and g(x)= 7x+b. You are asked to find f(g(x)). To do this, you must evaluate f(x) with g(x). When you do this you get f(x)=√7x+b. You now plug in the point values and simplify to get 36=28+b. Solve for b and you get choice 8, or **A**. Be careful to plug the point values in the end of the problem.

58) This problem tests your knowledge of reflections and where the corresponding points are reflected. The easiest way to do this problem is to draw a rough sketch of the reflection. The reflection is of x, y, and z. In the new quadrilateral, the perimeter sides are y and z. It is easy to see that the perimeter is 2y+2z, or 2(y+z), which is **choice K**. This problem is very easy, but make sure that you are reflecting across the right line, YZ.

59)This problem tests your understanding of the shape of a function graph that is odd. However, the problem is leading you to do the problem the long way, plugging in x values to see if f(-x)=-f(x). One very important concept that you should know is that odd functions, along with having the above rule, are also symmetric across the x axis. The only graph that displays this characteristic **is E**, the graph of the cubic.

60) This problem is just testing your understanding of logarithmic notation. You have to take this problem by steps. The first part is condensing the expression Log_2 24-log$_2$ 3 which becomes log$_2$ 8. This equals 3. Do not try to look at the whole equation including log$_5$ x. Once you know that the first part equals 3, you can easily solve the equation: log $_5$ x= 3, which is 5^{3}or 125, or **answer J**.

Notes

READING STRATEGY
By **Rajiv Raju**

If you can not find the reason to support an answer do not pick it.

The ACT Reading section tests your reading skill and speed. You will have to read the entire passage and understand it. Many of the questions can only be answered by going back to the passage and looking for evidence to support the answer. The passage always has the information to answer the question, but it may take time to find the information. Many students will not be able to finish the reading test in the allotted 35 minutes. If you have difficulty finishing this section, you might consider carefully reading three of the four passages and guessing on the fourth passage. Assuming that you are able to correctly answer all of the questions in three of the passages and assuming you get three of the ten questions correct on the fourth passage just from the laws of probability, you will have a raw score of 33 which corresponds to a scaled score of 30 based on the scoring chart in Preparing for the ACT. This may be a better score than what you might get if you rushed through all four of the passages without fully understanding them.

Here is the suggested strategy. **Read the entire passage-almost skim- as quickly as you can without dwelling on all the details.** You should however **be aware of where the details are located** so you can quickly find them when you answer questions. When you answer the questions, you should always go back to the passage to find evidence to support the correct answer. There may be a few general questions about the theme or tone of entire passage that may not require you to go back to the passage, but you should be going back to passage for most of the questions. When you answer the questions keep in mind that there is only one correct answer and the reason for the answer is always in the passage. No outside knowledge is needed and even the reasoning questions only require simple direct inference. If you can not find a specific reason in the passage to support an answer choice, then do not pick it as the correct answer. If you find any evidence for why an answer choice is wrong, eliminate the choice from consideration. **Do not think that an**

answer is correct for some reason that you do not see. This is time consuming but will increase your accuracy substantially. In your English class you may have been expected to interpret literature to find hidden meanings. These "hidden meanings" might be debatable. This is not a problem in English class since you can write a response to defend a debatable interptation. This kind of "deep interpretation" can get you in trouble on the ACT reading section. The ACT can never test you on debatable hidden meanings, since there can only be one right answer on a multiple choice test. **Never look for "hidden meaning" on the ACT reading test, just look at what is explicitly stated and keep interpretation to a minimum.**

If you can finish the test with this approach you should do very well. Even if you are unable to finish the test, you may still be able to get a respectable score if you do well on the portion of the test that you do complete. Remember to fill in all the answer choices for the questions that you did not have time for. You have a 25% chance of getting these questions right, as the reading section has four answer choices per question.

The next chapter goes through all 40 questions in the reading section of the booklet and illustrates how, in each case, the information in the passage supports the one correct answer and often contradicts the incorrect answer choices.

ACT READING EXPLANATIONS
By **Rajiv Raju**

1) This question is directly asking you to state the main idea of the paragraph. When you think of the main idea of this passage, think about themes that are relevant throughout the majority of the passage. The relationship between the Eugene and the narrator is the most prevalent theme. Choice C and D can be eliminated because, while the neighbors were mentioned, they were only talked about in the introductory paragraph and referred to in the last sentence. Since A and B are both about Eugene and the girl, you must identify which one provides the most valid statement about the passage. While choice A states correctly that the narrator had trouble starting the relationship, it is evident that the two "hit it off" quite quickly and didn't have trouble maintaining the relationship because of their mutual love for books. Therefore, **choice B** is the correct answer because it says that the passage concerns the process of making a new friend, which the narrator does, and also concerns the change that the narrator makes about thinking about the present more than the future.

2) For this question, you need to read through the answer choices and see which one is the valid statement based off the information in the passage. Choice F is wrong because it is evident that the narrator has never walked in Eugene's house in the last paragraph because she says she would like to one day. Choice G is wrong because it is clearly stated in the passage that both the narrator and Eugene like books. Choice H is wrong because it is stated in the first paragraph that Eugene's house was the only house on the block with a front yard and trees. **Choice J** is the correct answer because in the second to last paragraph, the narrator only states that she wishes to become a teacher.

3) This, like most questions on the reading section of the ACT, is an information question, or a question that gives you

statements and asks you to pick the valid one based off the information in the passage. Choice A is wrong because it is evident that the old couple weren't socially out going and spent most of their time together. Choice B is wrong because, while the father has tended the lawn, the flowers are no longer there, as indicated in the second paragraph. Choice D there is no comparison made between the employment of the old couple and Eugene's parents because we don't know if the old couple had jobs or not. **Choice C** is correct because it is stated in the passage that the old couple spent a lot of time together, evident by how they cared for each when they were sick, while Eugene's dad didn't even come home for dinner.

4) In this question you need to read the given lines(67-87) and interpret their purpose. After reading the lines and looking at all the answer choices, you see that they all deal with one thing: the family of the narrator, so you need to eliminate some choices that are irrelevant to the passage or are not the primary reason that the narrator wrote the lines. Choice G is one of these because no contrast is made between her parents and the couple because the parent's feelings towards each other aren't mentioned. Choice H is wrong because it is neither stated in the lines nor the passage that the narrator's friendship with Eugene has affected her family. Choice J is wrong because it is not stated in the passage that her parent's aspirations have changed over time, and we are to assume that her parents still wanted to live on a beach in Puerto Rico one day. **Choice F** is the correct answer because it is directly stated in the passage that the narrator's perspective based on her family had changed when she met Eugene, and she now thought of her future with him.

5) This question is also asking you to look at some given lines (30-31) and pick the valid choice. Choice A is wrong because it is not stated in the passage that the flowers were still growing, so you can't assume that. Choice B is wrong because it is never stated in the passage that the narrator watered the plants of old woman. Choice D is incorrect because it was not stated in the passage that the "weeds intertwined with the flowers. **Choice C** is correct because it is reasonable to infer the flowers were cut down because

Eugene's father spent a few days mowing the lawn to clear it out, and it was stated that only the grass remained.

6) This question is also asking you to pick the valid answer based off of the passage. Choice F is incorrect because it is explicitly stated in the passage that Eugene had spent time with the narrator on her fire escape before school started. Choice G is incorrect because Eugene did not seek out the narrator, rather, the narrator went out of her way to look for Eugene at school. Choice H is incorrect because it can be inferred that when Eugene noticed narrator, he was shy and because of this he didn't introduce himself. **Choice J** is correct because Eugene was shy around the narrator because he was nervous about reaching out, and he did notice her at school.

7) This question asks you to look at given lines(80-81) and pick the answer that provides the best explanation of those lines. Choice B is wrong because changing her opinion of her career path doesn't have anything to do with thinking more about the present than the future. Choice C is incorrect because it is not specifically stated in the passage that the narrator wanted to return to the island, though her parents did. Choice D is wrong because the narrators parents are unable or don't want to just go on a vacation to Puerto Rico, but rather buy a house there. **Choice A** is correct because it is stated in the passage that the narrator looked towards the future at her employment, but then her new friendship diverted her attention.

8) This question asks you to basically paraphrase the second to last paragraph of the passage. Choice F is wrong because the dream of living in Puerto Rico is not said to have been close. Choice G is wrong because it is a direct contradiction to what is stated in the passage as the other people in the building do have similar goals. Choice J is wrong because it is not stated in the passage specifically; rather, the narrator would rather go to college become a teacher than move back to Puerto Rico. **Choice H** correctly captures the essence of the last two paragraphs and is the correct answer.

9) This question asks you to answer a question based on information alluded to in the passage. Choice A is a direct contradiction to information given in the passage because the narrator said specifically that she could not hear the neighbors. Choice B is wrong because, although the author wished to tend the flowers. Choice C is only partially valid because, while the narrator could see the couple, she could not see them in the entire house. **Choice D** is the correct answer because the only time the narrator saw the couple during mealtimes in the kitchen in the description in the first paragraph.

10) This question asks you to paraphrase one of the paragraphs dealing with her feelings towards spying on Eugene. Choice F is wrong because the narrator, while she feels "joy" of a sort by spying on Eugene, she feels dishonest rather than suspicious. Choice H is correct because there is nothing in that paragraph of the passage that indicates that the narrator felt betrayed by spying on Eugene. Choice J is incorrect because while the narrator found it pleasurable to spy on Eugene, she did not feel less of him after she met him. **Choice G** is the correct answer because the narrator felt enjoyment when spying on Eugene, yet felt guilt and dishonesty when doing it as well.

11) This question is basically asking about the overall passage since the whole passage is about Eleanor Roosevelt and what she was like. Choice A is wrong because, although Eleanor Roosevelt was socially controversial, she was not quietly cooperative and it is even stated that she disagreed with her husband openly. Choice C is wrong because Eleanor was morally strong, but she contradicted traditions and "courted radicals". Choice D is incorrect because it is a contradiction to what is stated in the passage. Eleanor was far from moderate even though she was personally driven and she welcomed radical ideas. **Choice B** is correct because ER was politically courageous by openly arguing with FDR and was socially concerned, especially with racial and gender discrimination.

12) This question asks you to pick which choice is accurately stated in the passage regarding the question. Choice G is

wrong because it is not stated in the passage that ER gave political roles for women, even if she might have done so. Choice H is wrong because it is not stated in the passage that ER was alone in her "struggle" for social reform. Choice J is wrong because not once is there any mention of "powerful White House networks". **Choice F** is correct because it can be inferred that ER brought unpopular views to the forefront of politics especially in her fight against racial inequality.

13) This question is also testing your ability to pick that choice with the information that is NOT supported in the passage. Be careful to not get confused by finding the information that is supported by the passage, and waste precious time. Choice A, B, and C are all wrong because they are mentioned in the same paragraph as what every person should have. **Choice D** is correct because it is direct contradiction to information in the passage. It is stated that ER disliked involved(complex) theories and wanted effective action.

14) This question is testing your overall understanding of the passage because you really need to read the whole passage to understand ERs approach to social reform. Choice F is wrong because although ER was passionate about reform, it is specifically stated that she does not like theoretical reform. Choice G is incorrect because ER wanted action now and she was firm in her beliefs, so this is a direct contradiction to information given in the passage. Choice H is wrong because there is no evidence in the passage to say that ERs reforms were simplistic and she changed her views on isolationism soon after the FDR took office. **Choice J** is correct because it is stated in the passage that ERs approach was progressive because it was often controversial or defied traditions and that she was determined to make these reforms occur and used her roles as first lady to its fullest degree.

15) This question asks you to pick the answer choice that is directly supported by the passage. Choice A is a direct contradiction to information in the passage because it is stated that until ER came to the White House, the people weren't committed to social reform. Choice B is wrong because it is not stated in the passage that the nation was in a time of prosperity; in fact, the nation was in the middle of a

massive depression at the time! Choice C is wrong because it is a direct contradiction to information presented in the passage. Democracy was not spreading overseas; rather, communism and fascism was gaining popularity. **Choice D** is correct because it can be inferred from the information that before ER gained influence, people did not pressure the government to take care of the poor.

16) This question requires you to find the answer choice that restates the last paragraph. Choice F is wrong because it is not stated in the last paragraph that ER played "the game" only when she knew when she could win. In fact, it is stated that ER played "the game", win or lose. Choice H is wrong because it is not stated that ER placed her self in the position of president. Choice J is wrong because while it may be true, which it probably isn't, it is not mentioned in the last paragraph. **Choice G** is correct because it correctly restates the last paragraph and even includes key words that were present in the paragraph such as "agitators" and also states that she pursued justice in victory and defeat, which is also mentioned in this paragraph.

17) This question is asking you to pick the choice that makes the most sense as related to paragraph 3. Choice B is wrong because it is contradictory to information in paragraph 3. ER owned a school and co-owned a crafts factory. Choice C is wrong because there is no evidence in paragraph 3 on which you can come to the conclusion that ER had conflicting interests during her first year as first lady. Choice D is wrong because it can be reasonably inferred that the leadership positions described in paragraph 3 would prepare ER for life as first lady. **Choice A** is correct because it states that ERs successes in personal endeavors prepared her for her role because they were also leadership positions.

18) For this question, you need to understand the passage as a whole because it asks you to pick the answer that is best supported by the passage. Choice G is wrong because it is contradictory to information given in the passage because ER often brought up progressive and controversial topics as first lady. Choice H is wrong because it is not stated in the passage that ER had any personal columns or radio

broadcasts. Choice J is wrong because, while one of ERs principles was to lead a bloodless American revolution, it wasn't her primary principle. Rather, her primary principle was **Choice F**, or that every person should have a dignified and decent life. This is explicitly stated in the 7th paragraph.

19) For this question you need to look at the 8th paragraph for what ER thought the relationship between the people and the government should be. Choice A can be eliminated because it is a direct contradiction to ERs ideal of the unified citizens. Choice B is incorrect because ER believed that the citizens should step up and form their relationship with the White House with out the government's assistance. Choice D is incorrect because it is not stated in the passage that radio broadcasts and formal channels should be used to control the relationship between the White House and the citizens. **Choice C** is correct because it accurately states ER believed that *community,* or unified citizen, action was required for social reform.

20) This question asks you to put the given phrase in different terms while still keeping the same meaning in the context of the passage. Choice F is wrong because it is not stated in the passage that ER's adventure was individualist. Choice G is wrong because it is also not stated that ER was a team player over a leader; in fact, it can be inferred that ER liked to take the lead through her extensive use of her first lady powers. Choice J is wrong because it is not stated that ER didn't take criticism or politics very seriously. **Choice H** is correct because it is evident throughout ER's life that she loved politics, but often received and accepted criticism on her often controversial positions.

21) You need to read the whole passage and understand its layout to answer this question. Choice B is wrong because from reading the passage, it cannot be reasonably concluded that the author tried to show that the claims she made in the first paragraph are wrong; in fact, the whole passage seems to be supporting that claim. Choice C is wrong because not once are the narrator's parents mentioned in the passage. Choice D is incorrect because for one thing, the event is probably not recent since the narrator was five when it

happened and five-year olds can't write essays under most circumstances☺. Also it can be inferred that the lesson the narrator learned was very significant because it has apparently changed her entire view on life. **Choice A** is correct because the passage starts out with an assertion supported by a personal story. The story is used to show why the author has such an opinion on the topic mentioned in the first paragraph.

22) Look at the lines that are referred to(9-44) and analyze them. It is evident that the narrator is portraying a scared character that comes to a conclusion eventually. Since the question asks about mood, you have to pick a choice that would most likely be true under the given circumstances. Choice F is wrong because while the narrator has a steadily increasing amount of tension, it is not present during the whole anecdote. Choice G is wrong because it can be inferred that the narrator has a slowly increasing amount of tension as the shadow travels across her room. Choice J is wrong because there does not appear to be any elements of irony or humor in the excerpt. **Choice H** is correct because it supports the fact that the narrator has a growing feeling of tension, but that tension is dissipated when she finds out that the source of the "thing" is a passing car.

23) This question asks you to interpret the meaning of the third paragraph. Choice A is wrong because the narrator does not describe the nature of the object as much as the actions that the object is performing. Choice B is wrong because the narrator didn't do anything and all she did was observe the thing. Choice D is incorrect because the narrator does not speculate where the object came from. She is just observing its movements with detail. **Choice C** is correct because it accurately states what the narrator is doing: observing the thing and describing its doings with lots of detail.

24) For this question, you need to find the paragraph with the required information(paragraph 2). It is evident that the narrator didn't want to wake her sister when the thing came in because she was too scared to move. You have to pick the choice that most closely resembles this inference. Choice F is wrong because the narrator hadn't even talked to Amy at

all. Choice G is a direct contradiction to information in the paragraph because the narrator explicitly states that she cannot muster the charmed innocence of her sister. Choice H is wrong because it is not states that the narrator's sister Amy knew what the thing was. **Choice J** is the answer because it supports the claim that the narrator was scared because if the narrator was scared, she wouldn't want to attract the attention of the thing that was scaring her.

25) This is yet another question where you must identify the feeling of the narrator when a certain thing happened. Choice A is far from correct because if anything, the narrator would be relieved to find out what caused the thing that was causing her fears. Choice B is wrong because of the same reason: she wouldn't be unhappy if she found out the cause of the thing that is causing her tension. Choice C is wrong because it is evident that there is more that is gained than the narrator's ability to sleep at night because the rest of the essay is about how her outlook on life changed after this incident. **Choice D** is the right answer because the rest of the essay is pretty much about the insights on life that the narrator received from this conclusion.

26) This question is asking you to interpret what the metaphor referred to means in terms of the narrator coming to her conclusion. Choice F is wrong because there is no mention of monsters in the passage and this "fear" does not pertain to the metaphor given. Choice H is incorrect because although the metaphor has to deal with the boundary between inner and outer lives. Choice J is a contradiction to information in the passage because there was no bitterness when the narrator came to her conclusion and she was not leaving comforting memories. **Choice G** is correct because the conclusion she made about the "thing" was the time when the narrator crossed the boundary between the inner and outer world.

27) To answer this question, you need to understand the theme of the whole passage: The narrator comes to a conclusion and crosses the threshold between the interior world and fantasy, to the outside world and reality. Choice A is wrong because a story that the narrator has read has nothing to do

with the given phrase, which most reasonably refers to the "thing" that the narrator saw in her childhood. Choice B is wrong because of the same reason as above. Choice C is wrong because it is evident that the show of light that the narrator describes is contradictory to the outer world; rather, it is an element of the interior world. **Choice D** is correct because the show of light is most nearly a fantasy created by the mind, when really it is just a shadow of something in the outside world (the car, as the narrator found out).

28) The lines referred to (3-5), may seem hard to comprehend, but by reading them you should get the idea of what type of thought it is. Choice G is wrong because while the "self" (interior life) is mentioned many times in this excerpt, it is not referring to self examination. Choice H is wrong because the lines are focused on the "self", not analysis of nature. Choice J is wrong because it cannot be reasonably inferred that the "interior life" has debates with it self. **Choice F** is the correct answer because the lines mention how all the happenings revolve around the "self" and that these occurrences are deceptive. The words "blinds it and deafens it" relate to deceptive self-absorption.

29) This question is asking you to, like stated, paraphrase the given lines (5-8). Choice A is wrong because the lines do not state that the imagination lacks value, but it should be used in constructive ways. Choice B is wrong because lines 5-8 focus on the imagination, not reason. Choice D is incorrect for the same reason, and the words enrich is used in the wrong context. **Choice C** is correct because it accurately states, just like in the passage, that imagination shouldn't be used without focus on the real world, at least at some times.

30) This question is also asking you to paraphrase the given lines (77-80). The narrator is stating in the lines that she is relatively unimportant part of the world, considering how big it is. Choice F is wrong because, while the lines refer to how she as a child was unimportant, the lines do not say that adults are considered more important than children. Choice H is wrong because while it is stated that people could see or ignore the narrator, it is not stated whether it matters to her or not which one the people who pass her choose to do.

Choice J is wrong because she is not saying in those lines that she is less valuable than anyone. **Choice G** is correct because it accurately paraphrases the lines by saying she is a part of a very large world, along with many other people and things.

31) For this question you need to have a clear understanding of the passage to see which of the conclusions presented is valid. Choice A is wrong because there is no evidence in the passage to make the conclusion that important new theories will be accepted, no matter what. In fact, that seems contradictory to the passage because it seems new theories often have slim chances of survival, especially from new scientists. Choice C is wrong because it is evident from the passage that research into new theories is not respected in the scientific community, and it is even stated that Louis Frank's theory had opposition of 10000:1. Choice D is wrong because it is specifically stated in the passage that even scientists don't want to deal with new discoveries or theories. **Choice B** is the correct answer because it is explicitly stated in the last sentence of the passage that if Louis Frank was a scientist of a lesser standing, his theory wouldn't have been taken seriously. In other words, scientists of higher standings have a better chance of successfully introducing new and unusual ideas.

32) This question asks about feelings within a certain part of the passage, specifically the opinions of Frank's colleagues after he presented his comet idea. The main thing to understand is that Franks colleagues didn't think less of him after he presented his idea, and it is stated at the beginning of the third paragraph that his presentation probably only helped his career. Therefore, you can eliminate F and G because they say that the colleagues had lesser opinions of Frank and Sigwarth after they presented their theory, which is not true. The information in choice H is not supported in the passage, as nothing is said about Frank's colleagues thinking of him as someone who worked hard on his theory. **Choice J** is the correct answer because although the colleagues didn't take well to the new theory because they thought it was improbable, but that his research proved that there was definitely something bombarding the earth on terms with Frank's comet theory.

33) This is another question asking about the feelings of
someone in the passage. It is important to note that Frank
did not feel happy or proud after he presented his theory.
You can eliminate C and D because of this because in C, it
states that he was proud and in D it states that he was
satisfied. Choice A is wrong because there is no evidence in
the passage that states that Frank was treated badly after his
presentation. **Choice B** is correct because it is evident that
his coworkers no longer ridicule him because his research
has shown there is something on par with the thing in Frank's
theory that is bombarding the earth.

34) This question is asking what is implied by paragraph 4. The
quickest way to answer this question is to read the excerpt
and go through the answer choices to see which one best
describes what the excerpt is saying. Choice F is wrong
because there is no part before this paragraph where the
author criticizes other scientists. Choice G is incorrect
because it cannot be reasonably inferred that the author was
making any statement about the scientists' role in society.
Rather, he is most nearly stating that scientists do not like
change as much as the rest of the laymen. **Choice H** is
correct, however, because it states this exactly by saying
scientists "loath to embrace radically new ideas". Even
though you have found the answer that is surely correct, you
should ALWAYS look at all of the answer choices regardless.
By looking at Choice J, we can be sure it is wrong because it
in this paragraph there is no mention or comparison of
theoretical and practical scientific research.

35) This question is asking you to find specific information in the
passage, yet it does not give you a paragraph to at which to
look. Therefore, you should look at the first sentence of each
paragraph starting with the second paragraph (the first
paragraph is the introduction) until you find the information
that you need. This happens to be the sixth paragraph.
Choice B can be eliminated immediately because water
entering the atmosphere is not even mentioned in this
paragraph. The rest of the answer choices, however, are
information contained in the paragraph. While the
information in Choices C and D, the static on the

transmissions and the specks on the satellite images, caught the scientists attention during their research, the original project was about electrical activity, or the charged particles named plasmas, accompanying sunspots. **Choice A** is the correct answer.

36) This question asks you how a certain set of lines affects the argument presented in the paragraph. Choice F sounds like the correct answer because numbers are indeed provided earlier in the paragraph and the sentence stating that the planet is billions of years old supports the statement that the water level grows an inch every 10,000 years. However, you always need to look at the other choices no matter how correct the answer choice sounds. In this case, as it is in most cases, the other choices are wrong, but that is not always the case. Choice G is incorrect because it is not implied that the evidence given had limitations. Choice H is incorrect because it can be inferred that the main purpose of the paragraph and the specific lines is not to provide additional details about how big the comets are, even though those details are provided. Choice J is incorrect because, again, the purpose of the paragraph is not to give readers the sense of how old the planet is, even though it is stated that the planet is billions of years old. So **Choice F** is the correct answer.

37) This question asks you what the scientific community most nearly thought about the comet theory. Choice A is incorrect because it is implied that although scientists were skeptical, they did acknowledge that something was bombarding the atmosphere. Choice B is incorrect because it is stated that the scientists who were responsible for the comet theory were outvoted 10000:1. Choice C sounds correct because it can be inferred that the scientists did not agree fully with all the aspects of the small-comet theory, but that they were willing to consider that something was hitting the atmosphere on a regular basis. Again, we must look at Choice D to make sure that it isn't right. Choice D turns out to be incorrect because most scientists did NOT think that the comet theory was completely correct, but they were willing to consider it as a possibility. So **choice C** is the correct answer.

38) This question is asking you to analyze the given word and its sentence and answer in what context the word is used. Choice F is wrong because it is evident that the scientists agreed that something was hitting the atmosphere on par with the comet theory, regardless of whether it was comets or not. Choice G sounds correct because it can be inferred that although the scientists agreed that something was hitting the earth based on the information in the small-comet theory, they still weren't absolutely sure what was hitting the earth. Checking on the other answer choices, Choice H is wrong nothing is mentioned or can be inferred in the sentence about the practical value of the theory. Choice J is completely wrong because the methods that the Frank and Sigwarth use to collect evidence have nothing to do with the question whatsoever. **Choice G** is the correct answer.

39) This question asks you to rephrase what Richard Zare is saying. This is an example of a question where it is imperative that you read all of the choices. Choice A is wrong because although the term schizophrenic is used as a descriptive term, it is not meant literally. Choice B and C both sound right because they are contained in the excerpt of the passage. However, **Choice D** is the correct answer because it states that scientists have to maintain a balance of questioning and accepting current ideas. Choice B and C are both wrong because they are examples of what all scientists try to avoid being, according to Zare.

40) The question asks you to pick the answer choice that best supports the information given in the passage regarding the scientists' attitude towards their theory. The information is perfectly stated in one sentence at the beginning of the seventh paragraph. ("After a while their curiosity…grew into a preoccupation, then bordered on obsession.") Looking at the choices, the answer that best restates this sentence is **Choice H** because it is evident that the scientists became more and more captivated by the theory to which they could find no explanation.

ACT SCIENCE REASONING STRATEGY
by **Rajiv Raju**

No need to review your science text book for this section!

The science reasoning test presents scientific descriptions/data and tests your ability to analyze this information. Having science classes will help you develop the skill that this section tests, but you do not need to memorize any facts or formulas. All the information that you will need is presented to you in the test.

Of the 40 questions in the science reasoning test from the booklet, we found two questions that required the student to make common sense assumptions. In question 28, we have to make the assumption that liquids layer based on density. In question 37 we have to make the assumption that the deepest deposits are the oldest deposits. The information and assumptions needed to answer all the other 38 questions are explicitly stated in the test.

As with the Reading section, many students will not be able to finish this section. If you are having difficulty finishing this section, you may want to try and answer some questions without reading the entire passage. To prove that this works at least on some questions try the following test: Try to answer questions 8 to 13 by only looking at the graphs. Do not read any of the paragraphs. For question 8 look at Figure 1 and you should be able to answer the question even if you don't understand what S allotropes and SO_2 are. Now try question 9. Figure 4 has all the information needed to answer this question even if you do not know what reflectance is. Similarly questions 10, 11, and 12 can all be answered based on the graphs alone. In question 13, we actually have to know what reflectance is. Since the question refers to Study 1 we find can quickly find the definition of reflectance because it is in the first sentence of the paragraph dealing with Study 1 and is italicized with the definitions in parenthesis. At least in this case we are able to answer 5 of the 6 six questions without reading any text. Even the sixth question can be answered by looking up the definition and looking at the graphs. This technique will not always work, but it might be worth trying if you are running out of time. In passage one, for questions 1 to 7 we have to read the passage to answer the questions. In any case you should always fill in an answer for every question, even if it is a guess. Remember, there is no penalty for guessing on ANY of the ACT sections.

The recommended strategy for the science reasoning test is as follows:

If the passage has a **lot of text and few tables and graphs**, just **read the whole passage** as quickly you can and then answer the questions as you would with the reading section. When you answer the questions you must go back to the passage to find evidence to support your answer. If you find evidence to contradict a choice, eliminate it from consideration. There will always be evidence in the passage to support the correct answer. **Do not talk yourself into an answer that can not be explicitly supported in the passage.**

If you see a **lot of graphs and tables of data go straight to the questions** and try to answer as many of the questions as possible based on the data alone, reading the text only as needed. **Any important definitions will be italicized and easy to find.** The definition usually follows the italicized word. Once again, you must only pick the answers that can be supported by the data. In the sections with many graphs and tables, understanding every aspect of the concepts outlined is almost always not necessary. Your main objective is to answer the questions correctly, not to understand all of the jargon and concepts in the passage. Do not let the jargon scare you. The questions are usually easy. Sufficient information about the concepts can be deduced directly from the charts. What is most important in these chart-based passages is to understand the variables of the experiment and the effect of the variables on each other.

The next chapter goes through all 40 questions in the Science section of the booklet and illustrates how, in each case, information from the passage supports the one correct answer and often contradicts the incorrect answers. Remember, the ACT places trick answer choices in the test that the test makers know can be incorrectly inferred by the test takers. They know how our brains tick, in other words, at least with regards to test taking. So don't fall for the incorrect answer patterns. **The answer is ALWAYS explicitly stated in the passage, or can be reasonably inferred from the data given.**

ACT SCIENCE EXPLANATIONS
By **Rajiv Raju**

Passage 1

1) For this problem, you actually have to look in the passage to find the answer, specifically to find the time required to replicate a gene, which happens to be 15 minutes. Since the question is asking how many complete genes can be replicated within 50 minutes, all you have to do is some simple math to find that 3 genes can be replicated in 45 minutes. Note that although there is time left, there is not enough time to replicate another full gene so the only correct **answer is B**.

2) For this problem again you have to look at the reading under Student 3. According to this theory, the replication process moves clockwise. The problem is giving you an example of this, starting with G, and you have to find the THIRD replication. If you follow the directions, this is easy and you should get Gene X, or **choice J**. Be careful however, not to pick the consecutive gene just when you figure out how to do the problem.

3) You have to look at the reading yet again for this problem. The question is asking which of the students supports the idea posed by the question, which is, that replication can start with any gene. Luckily, it turns out that the answer for this question is in the first sentence of every paragraph for the students. Using this insight, you can quickly eliminate A and B because those students' theories postulate that the replication can only start with specific genes. While D has the correct answers, it also contains Student 2, which is wrong. Therefore, **C** is the correct answer, which is Student 3 and Student 4.

4) For this problem, you need to understand two key pieces of information from the passage: the replication process takes 15 minutes and that replication in student A's theory starts with X

and ends with F. The problem asks which gene will not be replicated if the process is interrupted after 45 minutes following the constraints of Student A's hypothesis. Since 3 genes are replicated after X, the only gene that is not replicated is Gene G, which is answer **choice F**. Be careful not to start with gene F and from there, as the information from student A can be easily misunderstood.

5) This question is asking the same question as problem #4 except it is asking about student 2 and tells that the replication is interrupted after 30 minutes. By following the instructions of student 2 and starting with either X or F(then replicating 2 genes), we can see that neither gene A or gene S is replicated. However, only A is in the answer choices, so the answer is **A**.

6) This problem is quite easy if you realize that this problem is problem 3 reworded. Since it is asking which students would agree that replication would end with gene A, all you need to do is look back and see that students 1 and 2 say that the replication ends with specific genes, which are either F or X. Only 3 and 4 say that replication can begin and end with any gene. Therefore, the answer is **J**.

7) By adhering to the constraints set by student 1, you start with gene X and move one gene, 15 minutes at a time until you get past gene A. This means 4 genes(X,R,S,A) have been replicated. 4 times 15 minutes is 60 minutes so the answer for this straightforward problem is **D**.

Passage 2

8) For this question, you simply need to find the graph that corresponds to study 1 and interpret the graph. You can cross out H and J because the S allotrope is increasing only. Out of choice F and G, you need to look at SO_2's graph. The graph increases at first, but then decreases. **Choice G** is the only choice that gives this description of SO_2's graph and the correct description for S's graph

9) For this question you have to look at the corresponding graph for study 3. The question is very simple since there are only two pieces of data that you need to look at. From looking at the graph it is very easy to see that large plumes always give off a reflectance that is less than of smaller plumes. It never has greater reflectance than the smaller plumes. **Choice C** is the answer to this question.

10) For this question you need to carefully read the correct curve on the correct graph and estimate a value from the graph. Find the corresponding graph for study one and look at .40 on the wavelength axis. See at what value of reflectance that white S passes over this wavelength. The reflectance is about .2, which is **choice H**.

11) For this question you look at the graph for the Pele crater floor in study 2. You need to compare these similar graphs to one of the allotrope graphs from study 1. The Brown S graph is the closest to the graph of Pele, and this is **choice D**.

12) This question is asking you to do some simple linear extrapolation, or extending of the graph. Since .61 is very close to the end of the graph on the x axis, .60, you should find the answer choice with the closest reflectance values to those at .60 uM, Large: aprox. 0.5 Small: aprox. 0.9. Therefore, **choice H** is the answer.

13) For this question, you need to look at the graph corresponding to study 1 and the definition of reflectance, which is the fraction of light that strikes a surface that is reflected by that surface. This pertains to a specific wavelength. Choice A is wrong because it only accounts for the 2% that is LEFT. Choice C is wrong because it accounts only for the 2% left and it says that it reflects all visible light when reflectance only pertains to a specific wavelength. Choice D is also wrong because of this. **Choice B** is the only correct answer because it has the correct wavelength and the correct percentage of reflectance: 98%.

Passage 3

14) For this problem you need to look at the corresponding graph for experiment 1. The question asks you what the time constant is for a value that is not present on the chart. Fortunately, they are not asking for a specific number, which makes this question much easier. Find where 7.6 Volts would be, which is between 0.0 and 8.4. For the voltage to be 7.6, the time must be less than 12 seconds, which is **choice F**. All the other choices are wrong because they list the time constants for voltages greater than 7.6.

15) For this problem you need to look at table 2. The question asks you to do some extrapolation with the data given. It asks you to find the time it would take to reach across a 6 volt capacitor for a given capacitance, whose value is on the chart. The question asks for 1.5×10^{-6}, when the data on the chart only goes up to 1.2×10^{-6}. Immediately you can eliminate choices A and B because they are less time than 1.2×10^{-6}. There is a .3 increase between 1.2 and 1.5. If you notice on the chart, there is a .3 increase in capacitance between .3 and .6, and the time increase is 2.1. There for, for every $.3 \times 10^{-6}$ increase in capacitance, there is a 2.1 second time increase. You can add this time to 8.3 seconds and get 10.4. The closest answer to this is answer **choice C**, 10.5 sec.

16) This question is simply asking for the two variables in the chart in experiment 3, which is one of the easiest questions you will encounter on the science section of the ACT. On the chart there is resistance and the time to reach 6 V across the capacitor. If you look through the choices, the only choice with both of these variables is **choice J**.

17) This question just requires a little common sense. Since they are asking which circuit would only measure the voltage across the resistor, you should look for the choice where the line labeled "V", or the voltmeter, only goes around the resistor. According to figure 1, the resistor is the squiggly line at the bottom of the circuit. If you look at **choice A**, the line labeled V is only surrounding the squiggly line, which is the resistor, so this is the answer.

18) This question is asking which set of values for capacitance and resistance will cause the least time for the voltage to change. If you look at the table for experiment 2 and 3, you see that as both capacitance and resistance increase, the time required for the voltage to travel increases. So picking the lowest values for both of these will yield the least time. **Choice F** is the correct answer because out of all the answer choices, it gives the lowest values for BOTH capacitance and resistance. While choice G may have the same value of capacitance, it has a higher value of resistance, and vice versa for choice H. Choice J is the completely opposite answer for this question, as it gives the highest values.

19) This question is basically asking what is the relationship you found between capacitance and time you found in question 18. As capacitance increases, time increases. The hypothesis presented in 19 is true, so you can eliminate choices C and D. In choices A and B, however, there is a trick. The choices are essentially giving the same information, but choice A is listing the wrong experiment. Capacitance was not tested in experiment 1, but only in experiment 2. **Choice B** gives the accurate information and the correct experiment, so it is the correct answer.

Passage 4

20) In this problem, they tell you the tables of which to refer. You need to see the overall relationship present by the two charts. First, on table 2, you see that if you increase the amount of sucrose, the amount of heat released increases. These two charts may not seem alike at all, but you need the information in both to answer the question. You use table 1 to relate the heat released to the change in water temperature. The information is not in successive order, so do not be tricked into picking H just because that is how the information appears on table 1. If you match up the heat released and the change in water temperature and put it in successive order, you see that as the amount of heat released increases, the change in water temperature also increases and only increases. This is **choice F**.

21) This problem is asking you to represent the answer to the previous question in a graph. Because you found that as the amount of heat released increases, the change in water temperature increases, you should find a graph that has a constant positive slope since a direct proportion that is increasing has a consistently positive slope. Choice A is incorrect because while it is increasing, the graph levels off at a certain point. Choice C is incorrect because it shows the graph having a negative slope. Choice D is incorrect because it shows the graph level at first and then having a negative slope after a certain point. **Choice B** is the correct answer because it is a line with a positive slope that is always increasing.

22) This question asks you to evaluate the relationship between the two variables on table 2: the amount of sucrose and the heat released, and asks what happens to the amount of heat released if the amount of sucrose is halved. Since the upper four values (.5 to 4.0) of sucrose are in increments on twice the previous value, it is easy to see this relationship. If the amount of sucrose is halved, then the heat released is approximately halved as well. Choice A is wrong because it is the opposite of what would happen if the amount of sucrose was decreased. Choice H is wrong because ¼ is not the value by which the heat released is decreased. Though choice J correctly states that the amount of heat released would decrease, it does not give the correct factor of decrease (1/2). **Choice G** is the correct answer because it says that the amount of heat released would decrease and it gives the correct factor of decrease.

23) This question is asking you to put in order the foods relative to their amounts of heat released considering 1 gram of food. By looking at table 1, since all the foods are shown in 1 gram, it is easy to put them in order of heat released. However, you must also account for sucrose, which is in table 2. In table 2, you must find the value of heat released for 1 gram of substance, which is 16.0 kJ. By putting these all in order, you get: Potato, Egg, Bread, Sucrose, and Cheese. This is answer **choice A**.

24) For this problem you don't specifically need the information given in table 2, but you need to use it to realize that the amount of heat released relative to a food sample added is a linear proportion. Table 2 indicates a linear proportion with the property that as the amount of sucrose doubles, the amount of heat released doubles as well.   If you look at table 1, you see that the mass of potato is 1 gram. The question asks for the heat released for 5.0 grams of potato. All you have to do is multiply the amount of heat released for 1 gram of potato, 3.2 kJ, by 5, which is 16.0 kJ. Of the answer choices, this value is closest to choice H, 15 kJ, so the answer is **H**.

Passage 5

25) This question is asking you to analyze the graph in figure 1. However, the question is also asking you what happens when the temperature *decreases* from 10 to 0 degrees. This means that you need to interpret the graph backwards. Following the graph backwards, you see that it is increasing until about 4 degrees, but then starts decreasing until it reaches 0(degree symbol needed for these numbers). **Choice D** is the correct answer because it accurately states this. Choice A is wrong because the graph does not just increase because it reaches a peak and then decreases. Choice B is wrong because that answer would be interpreting the graph in the wrong direction because at first the graph is increasing. Choice C is wrong because it is the exact opposite of what the graph does, which is increase, then decrease.

26) For this problem, you need to compare the densities of solids and liquids in table 1. Since the hypothesis tells you that every solid compared to every liquid is greater in density, you must find the liquid with the greatest density and compare it with the densities of the solids. Mercury is the densest liquid in the chart, with a density of 13.59 g/cm^3. You can see that its density is greater than any solid on the table because the greatest density, Lead, is only 11.34 g/cm^3. You can get rid of H and J because the hypothesis is wrong. Choice F states the hypothesis is correct, but says that lead has a density greater than any liquid, which is a direct contradiction to the information presented on the table. **Choice G** is the correct

answer because it gives an accurate statement and states the hypothesis is wrong.

27) This problem requires you to make a very simple interpretation of the linear graph in figure 2. It asks you what happens as temperature increases, and it is easy to see that the graph decreases as temperature increases because of the negative slope. Therefore, the answer to this simple question is **B**, because the graph only decreases. Choice A is the exact opposite of the graph, and choices C and D describe a graph that is not linear.

28) For this question, you need to know that lower density substances are higher up in a solution. This is one of the rare cases where you need to have prior knowledge for the science reasoning test. If you look on the table with the densities, you see that ethyl ether has a density of .71 and that mercury has a density of 13.59. From the information given in the question you find that water has a density of .9971. From this information and the rule that lower densities are higher up in a solution, the correct solution would have: ethyl ether first, water second, and mercury third. This is **choice F**.

29) This question is very easy, but very easy to be tricked in as well. First, you need to find the density of water at 4 degrees Celsius, which is 1.000 g/cm^3. However, the question asks you the density when there is 100 grams of water. Now all you have to do is some simple multiplication, because 1 x 100 is 100, obviously. The answer is **C**. Don't be tricked by finding the density for only 1 gram of water, which is choice A. Choice B and D cannot be reasonably derived from the information given.

Passage 6

30) For this question, you need to look at the graph corresponding to study 4. By looking at the graph key, you can see that the line with squares going through it denotes frugigroves. If you look at the graph, the line for frugivores is steadily decreasing. **Choice F** is the correct answer because it correctly states this correlation. Choice G and H are wrong because the graph is

consistently going downwards; it does not change its relative correlation to change the sign of the slope.

31) For this question, to need to look at figure 3 evaluate each answer choice to see if it contains valid information based off of the graph. It is safe to assume that the number of captures is directly proportional to the populations of the animals Choice A is wrong because, while the population of hummingbirds is increasing, the population of insectivores is decreasing drastically. Choice B is wrong because the population of hummingbirds increased. Choice C is wrong because it is the exact opposite of the information presented in the graph: the population of insectivores did not increase, it decreased and the population of hummingbirds did not decrease, it increased. **Choice D** is correct because it accurately states that the population of insectivores decreased and that the population of hummingbirds increased.

32) For this problem, you need to look at figure 1, the graph for study 1, and do some linear interpolation with the given value of 75 meters to find the change in AGTB. Since 75 meters is between 70 and 80 meters on the graph, you can see that the change would be about less than -2 but greater than -3. The only value in the answer choices that fits in these restrictions is -2.6, or **choice G.** Be careful not to pick choice J because the values for the change in AGTB are negative.

33) For this problem, you need to see which choice is a reasonable explanation for the constant AGTB. Choice A and B can be eliminated because increasing or decreasing the AGTB would obviously not yield a constant average AGTB. **Choice C** is correct because increasing and decreasing the AGTB at the same time can keep the average AGTB constant. Choice D is wrong because the study was conducted in the forest and increasing the AGTB would not yield a constant AGTB. It is easy to see that many ACT questions just require a little common sense.

34) This is one of the few questions where you have to do some reading of the passage(excluding the conflicting scientists passages). You need to look at the thesis, which is generally in the introductory paragraph, to find the prediction of the

researchers. You need to look at the slope of the graphs to answer this question. Since the researcher's hypothesis is supported by data in studies 1 and 2, you can eliminate choices F and G. Choice H is wrong because the graph for frugivores validates the hypothesis that animal populations would decrease with fragmentation. **Choice J** is the correct answer because it is least consistent with the hypothesis because the population of hummingbirds is increasing, when the hypothesis states that the population of animals would decrease with fragmentation.

35) This problem is very simple, but it is easy to be tricked. They are asking how many insectivores would be trapped if 10, 000 hours were spent every year trapping birds. The graph in study 4 is in units of 1,000 hours per year. First you need to find the amount of insectivores trapped in year two for 1,000 of trapping, which is 80 insectivores, and multiply that value by 10 to see how many would be caught with 10,000 hours of work. This would be 800 insectivores, or **choice C.** Choice A is the trick because that is the answer that is presented on the graph. However, as stated before, the graph is in units of 1,000 hours of trapping per year.

Passage 7

36) For this question you need to look at the information given and compare it to the information given on the figures to find the best answer. A good place to start is matching up all the pieces of information on one chart. If you look at Table 1, you see that gray C is the closest to the percent volumes of sand, silt, and clay, with 31.7, 33.6, and 34.7 respectively. While the closest answer appears to be Gray C, you must look at figure 1 to make sure. Sure enough, the resistivity of gray till C is a little less that 100, which is close to 85 ohms, and the CO_2 content is a little above 20 mL/g, so the answer is **choice H**.

37) For this question, you need to do some reading of the introductory paragraph. From reading this, you find that it is indirectly alluding to the fact that older glaciers are lower underground. This should also be common sense for most people and can be considered one of the few things that they

must know for this test. With this information, it is easy to say that **choice D**, or Gray till D, is the answer because it is the deepest glacier.

38) For this question you need to look at the resistivity part of figure 1 and compare the resistivity graph of sand and gravel to that of the till layers. It is easy to see that sand and gravel has a higher resistance than any of the till layers, so the answer is **choice G**. Choice F is wrong because it is the complete opposite of the information presented in the graph, which states that sand and gravel had the highest resistivity. Choice H is wrong because it is not supported in the figure at all as no two sections have the same resistivity. Choice H is wrong because sand and gravel's resistivity is considerably higher than that of bedrock.

39) The simplest way to do this problem is to draw a line from the approximate end of the bedrock graph and see in which section it has the closest intersection. If you do this, you find that olive green and gray till have resistivities most liked bedrock. Therefore, answer is **choice C.**

40) This question asks you to look at Figure 1 and at the CO_2 data. Since the question tells you that data was collected at a site where the CO_2 content was much greater than any till, all you have to do is look for the area where CO_2 reaches its highest point. This is between 30 and 40 on the graph or approximately 35. Therefore, you need to find an answer choice greater than 35 mL/g, and the only answer choice that satisfies this **Choice J,** greater than 35 mL/g.

Notes

ACT WRITING (ESSAY) STRATEGY
By **Silpa Raju**

The ACT writing test is optional, but most competitive colleges require it. The score you receive on the essay will not affect your composite score or the English score. You will get an additional Essay score (2-12) as well as a Writing score which is a combination of your English score and Essay score.

You will have 30 minutes to complete the essay, so work quickly. **If you do not write a long essay you will not get a good score**. According to the official ACT booklet, <u>Preparing for the ACT</u>, your essay will be graded by the following guidelines:

"Your essay will be evaluated on the evidence it gives of your ability to do the following:

- express judgments by taking a position on the issue in writing prompt;
- maintain a focus on the topic throughout the essay;
- develop a position by using logical reasoning and by supporting your ideas;
- organize ideas in a logical way; and
- use language clearly and effectively according to the conventions of standard written English" (Pg. 10, <u>Preparing for the ACT</u>).

With this rubric in mind, let's go over some basic essay writing techniques. Keep in mind that not all of these will work for everyone since everyone works differently, but they're worth trying out.

Pick a side
There's no "in the middle"- if you want a good score, you better pick one side. However, in order to get a high score, it is necessary to anticipate and **respond to potential counterarguments** while still focusing on one side.

To plan or not to plan?

Preparing for the ACT recommends brainstorming before beginning to write. Our recommendation is to limit your planning to a minute and produce three examples. You can not afford to plan too long, since to get a high score you have to write a long essay. If you haven't thought of enough examples in your plan time, it would be a good idea to just begin writing and see where it takes you. If you haven't thought of all your examples by the time you're finished with your introduction paragraph leave blanks in the sentences in your introduction to fill in later.

Five-paragraph it

A basic five paragraph essay will take you far on the ACT writing test, though it certainly isn't totally necessary. Be sure to have some sort of introduction and conclusion, and preferably three examples. But if you can't manage to think of three examples or five paragraph essays aren't you thing, you can organize it differently. But if you're looking for the simplest way to organize your essay, this is the way to go.

Stay on topic

The score you receive primarily is dependent on the amount of information you present to support your side, and also how effectively you present it. Therefore, your essay should be as long as you can make it while still relevant. Show an organized flow of thought with supporting examples. Try not to digress.

Introductory Paragraph

Think of a couple of generalized sentences for the introduction which you can fill in with your examples. Here's an illustration:

Happenings from _____, _____, and _____ are prime examples that support this perspective.

You should come up with your own "canned" sentence. Make sure it has some good vocabulary and sentence structure.

Don't fill in the blanks with totally specific examples. In the introduction use general categories, like "my personal life", "history" or "literature". Save the more specific details for later paragraphs.

You can also pre write a good "canned" sentence to use in the concluding paragraph that you can customize for the examples you happen to use for the essay. This will give your essay at least two sentences with good vocabulary and sentence structure, which should help you get a higher essay score.

A Final Note

This may seem obvious, but after each example be sure to point out exactly how it supports your position. Bluntly stating this will illustrate that you have made a clear, strong connection between the position you hold and your examples.

Similarly, in the concluding paragraph you should explicitly state why all of your examples support your position. **You do not get any extra points for being subtle. Do not hesitate to restate the obvious**.

Notes

Notes

Notes

Notes

2359548

Made in the USA